THE BEST PUBS IN YORKSHIRE

ALSO BY BARRIE PEPPER

Pubs of Character in Yorkshire

Old Inns and Pubs of Leeds

A Haunt of Rare Souls — the old inns and pubs of Yorkshire

Sincere thanks are due to many members of CAMRA who have helped with both recommending pubs for this book and giving me their views and opinions on others. The final selection is mine alone. In particular I would like to thank the following: Joan Hewitt, Bob Hopkins, Bill Park, Stuart Sturrock, Richard Thompson, Colin Waite, Alan Walker, Malcolm Walker and Colin Wilson, as well as many licensees who have been ever helpful, and finally, whoever talked me into buying a word processor.

Barrie Pepper

THE BEST PUBS IN

Yorkshire

INCLUDING CLEVELAND & HUMBERSIDE

Barrie Pepper

Illustrated by Phil Evans

ALMA BOOKS

IN ASSOCIATION WITH THE CAMPAIGN FOR REAL ALE

Author: **Barrie Pepper**
Design: **Opus**
Illustrations: **Phil Evans**
Cartography: **Perrott Cartographics**
Cover photograph of the Spotted Cow, Malton, courtesy of Joshua Tetley & Son Ltd. Back cover of the Whitelocks, Leeds, courtesy of William Younger and Co.
Typeset and printed by: **Cambridge University Press**
ISBN **1–85249–101–9**
Published by **Alma Books Ltd.,** *a wholly-owned subsidiary of the Campaign for Real Ale Ltd., 34 Alma Road, St Albans, Herts.*

CONTENTS

FOREWORD

Yorkshire has been too much maligned for far too long. Because Southerners need somewhere to condescend to since they lost the empire they portray us as a rough tribe, living in back-to-backs on black puddings, and pulling the lining of our flat hats down our noses every time we pick them.

All lies. We don't bother to point it out. We're folk of few words and most of those are "bugger off". Besides, if we told the honest truth, that the Yorkshireman is humanity's finest flowering and the Broad Acres the best and most beautiful part of the country, then everyone would want to come. We'd be too throng wi'folk to move.

Barrie Pepper gives the game away in his excellent guide to the Best Pubs in the Best Part of the Best Country in the World. Quite rightly he's dealing with the real Yorkshire and includes the bits which are at present occupied territory in Humberside, Lancashire, Cleveland and Cumbria. This isn't quiche country. It's the real world of real industry, real people and real ale.

Picking the best is an impossible task. He's modestly limited himself to a couple of hundred. Yet this opens up the exciting prospect of trying them all out and comparing and contrasting his pick with yours. On the whole I approve. If we meet up in any of them I'd love to buy you a drink. If only I weren't a Yorkshireman, and in any case precluded from such bribery by electoral law. You can, however, buy me one.

Enjoy, as the Americans say. Feel as proud to be in God's Own Country as He does Himself. More power to your elbow As you bend it to sup up, drink us Yorkshire toast:

Ere's ter us an all on us
Me an all
May we nivver want nowt
Non on us
Nor me nawther

Austin Mitchell

INTRODUCTION

How do you select the best pubs in Yorkshire? The task is an impossible one. To start with how do you decide how many there are? To this extent my task has been made easier by the limitations placed on me by the size of this guide. So let us say there are 200 "best" pubs to be chosen from something just over 5,000 in the county. It is easy to rule out many of these but that simply reflects a personal view, for however bad we may think a pub is the fact is that it is open and selling beer and somebody may regard it as the best pub in the world. Perhaps the landlord does.

So the choice becomes essentially a personal one. I sought advice because I have not been in all the pubs in Yorkshire to assess their value. Such a task is not only impossible but pointless as well. Pubs change for any number of reasons and what is today's "best" pub may well be dropped from consideration when, for example, the landlord moves on. Another may move up the list with a fresh licensee, some sensitive alterations by the brewery or a change in the beers on sale. Who can tell in these days of takeovers if todays Nectar XXXX Ale will taste as good tomorrow when the tiny Dales brewery is owned by some Australian predator who wouldn't know a pint of good ale if he drowned in it. Which is not a bad idea.

Certain considerations are essential. The pub must sell real ale, cask conditioned beer, call it what you will; and it must be kept and served well. Then the pub must have other qualities and my benchmark has been for it to do well what it sets out to do. If its forté is good food then it must serve very good food. If atmosphere and conversation is what it is all about then that must be pre-eminent. Walkers' pubs must cater for walkers, locals look after locals and ale houses must shine so far as beer is concerned. If a mix of these various qualities is attempted then they must all be done well. That was my manifesto.

PERSONAL CHOICE

I therefore, as the legal eagles would have it, take full and absolute responsibility for the choice of pubs in this guide. I know I will upset many landlords who I hope will remain my friends, and I know many people will argue that I should have included their particular local rather than, well, you know where. The worthy burghers of one town will go for my jugular for missing it out completely and I shall be accused of favouring some others. My confession is that I like all the pubs in this guide and many more besides and I have tried to shake out a fair geographical balance and not favour any one brewery's products whilst attempting to include all the various types of pubs. *Mea culpa.*

Yorkshire is very much a county of chauvinist thought and I was brought up to believe that there is precious little in this world that has been created or invented that saw light outside the broad acres. But, surprisingly, it can make no claims to have given birth to either beer or the public house. If to anyone, the credit should go to the Egyptians for one and the Romans for the other. But beer has been brewed here for at least 2000 years and the county does claim both the oldest pub in England – the Bingley Arms at Bardsey (qv) – and the highest – the Tan Hill Inn on the Durham borders. And the pub, which is essentially an English institution, comes into its own in Yorkshire.

There is a wide selection of all types of pubs in the county; the gin palaces of the great cities as well as the downtown street corner boozers, whilst the Dales have their village inns and the main highways their road houses. And Yorkshire has its own unique style of pub. It comes from the West Riding in the "house style" with its central drinking area and rooms leading off. Good examples of this are the Garden Gate in Leeds (qv) and the White Lion in Sheffield (qv). Another type of pub often found in Yorkshire is the "shop style" where a counter running parallel to the front of the house is the main bar, as in the Albion in Leeds (qv) and the Mason Arms in Doncaster (qv).

PUBS UNDER THREAT

The public house is under threat from a number of sources. Yorkshire is not isolated in this respect and perhaps to some extent has been sheltered from the worst ravages of the past few years. The big brewers have sold off many pubs in the urban areas, some to the free trade and, of late following changes in planning law, to become shops and other retail establishments.

We are fortunate that the vast stretch of Yorkshire that covers the Dales, the Moors and the Wolds has mostly public houses in private ownership – the free trade – and they are practically take-over resistant. But there are predators about and the effects of legislation which will follow the recent Monopolies and Mergers Commission report on the supply of beer has yet to be seen. For the moment we must follow the advice of Yorkshire's most famous Prime Minister, Herbert Henry Asquith, and "wait and see."

Barrie Pepper

HOW TO USE THIS GUIDE

This guide is about pubs in Yorkshire, that is to say the real Yorkshire of the three ridings and the City of York. So in it you will find entries from areas such as Cleveland and Humberside that were created by the carve-up of local government in 1974; and there are others in places that were snatched from Yorkshire to become part of Lancashire, Durham and Greater Manchester.

For convenience the guide has been divided into six areas with the East Riding taking in Hull, Holderness, the Wolds and the coastal strip as far north as Flamborough. The North Riding has the rest of the county's magnificent coastline, Teesdale, Swaledale and Wensleydale, the North York Moors and much of the Plain of York. The City of York is exactly what it says it is and all the entries are within the boundaries of the former county borough.

The vast West Riding which stretches from Bawtry in the south-east to Sedbergh which is now in Cumbria, has been broken into three divisions. The northernmost sector, The Dales, covers Nidderdale, Wharfedale, Ribblesdale, Craven and those places north of a line running from Tadcaster, through Harrogate and Ilkley to the Lancashire border. Central Yorkshire covers the big cities of Leeds and Bradford with Wakefield and the wool towns and includes some splendid country around Holmfirth and Haworth. South Yorkshire takes in Sheffield, Rotherham and Doncaster and is a much more attractive part of the world than is often imagined.

HOW TO USE THIS GUIDE

The practical information for each pub is given in the form of symbols as shown below:

---

food is available as specified. This always means full meals unless otherwise indicated. Many pubs do not serve meals late in the evening, so check by phone if you wish to eat late.

---

a garden, or where specified, other outdoor area for drinking – occasionally this will just be tables on the pavement.

---

a family room or area without a bar is provided where the licensee will allow children accompanied by a parent or other responsible adult. In pubs where meals are served, children may be confined to the dining area, and thus be expected to have a meal. Check with staff.

---

the type of acommodation is specified, but no prices are given. Check by phone for availability.

---

real ales are listed with beers from independent breweries as well as national brands. For full details of local beers see the brewery section on p 14 or consult CAMRA's Good Beer Guide.

---

nearest British Rail station (within one mile).

WHAT IS REAL ALE?

Real ale is a definition accepted by the Concise Oxford Dictionary. It is also known as traditional draught beer or cask-conditioned beer. Real ale is brewed from malted barley, using pure water and hops, and fermented by top-fermenting yeast. At the end of fermentation the beer is allowed to condition for a few days and is then racked into casks, often with the addition of priming sugar and a handful of dry hops for aroma. The beer continues to "work" or ferment in the cask while a clearing agent called finings drags the yeasty deposits to the floor of the cask. The beer is neither filtered nor pasteurised and must not be served by any method using applied gas pressure.

Real ale can be served straight from the cask and many country pubs still use this method, while some special winter brews in town pubs are often dispensed from a cask on the bar. But most real ale is drawn – hence the word "draught" – by a suction pump from the pub cellar. The pump is operated either by a handpump, a tall lever on the bar, or by an electric pump. Electric pumps are rare in the south of England but are used widely in the Midlands and the North.

Real ale should be served at a temperature of 55–56 degrees F (12–13 degrees C). This is a cool temperature that brings out the best characteristics of a top-fermented beer. It is a higher temperature than those used for serving lager beers, but it is pure mythology that real ale is "warm".

PUB HOURS

In August 1988 the British Government made long-overdue changes to pub licensing laws, which had been severely restricted since the First World War. Pubs can now open Monday to Saturday from 11 am until 11 pm. But individual licensees can choose which hours they wish to open between 11 in the morning and 11 at night. They will choose their hours to suit their trade. Many pubs now display their opening hours on the exterior. Hours are not given for individual pubs in this guide. Most of them have elected to keep to the "traditional" hours, however it is likely that pubs in tourist areas, eg. York, or areas of high urban concentration will stay open in the afternoon, especially in the summer. During the winter months it is likely that many of these pubs will keep to the old hours and will close between 3 pm and 5.30 or 6 pm. Sunday hours have been only slightly extended: the standard hours are 12 noon to 3 pm and 7 pm to 10.30 pm.

CHILDREN IN PUBS

You cannot drink alcohol in a pub below the age of eighteen years (although at sixteen, children with adults may drink beer, wine or cider with a meal). You can go into a pub at fourteeen but you can drink only non-alcoholic products. Licensees tend to be extremely strict on "under-age" drinking, since they can be prosecuted and lose their licences to trade. Children of all ages can go into pubs that have rooms set aside as "family rooms". They can also eat in pubs that have rooms used as restaurants. If a pub in this guide is shown to have a beer garden then children can use this facility but if the garden is reached via the pub it is wise for parents or guardians to ask permission to take the children through the licensed area.

THE BREWERS

The drinkers of Yorkshire are fortunate that beers from more than 60 breweries are on regular sale in their pubs as well as many guest beers that flow in from all parts of the country. There are 29 breweries in the county alone ranging from some of the nation's biggest that are off-shoots of the massive combines to tiny home-brew pubs. Tetley Bitter is the world's best selling cask conditioned beer and is brewed in Leeds within one mile of the Ale House brewery, housed in a small room above an off-licence shop. There are regional independents and some smaller firms who have flourished in the real ale revival. Between them they brew more then 80 regular beers from the low gravity milds to a claimant for the world's strongest beer.

Beers on sale in pubs in this guide are listed below with some indication of their characteristics, and it must always be recognised that this is a subjective and often personal view. The original gravity of each beer is also given. This is a measure of its strength and is used to calculate excise duty. The term is related to the amount of fermentable materials at the beginning of any brew. An original gravity of 1040 would indicate that forty parts of fermentable matter such as malt and sugar have been added to 1000 parts of water. It is not an absolute measure of strength but a good indication. The alcoholic strength of beer depends also on the gravity level to which the beer is allowed to ferment down to, or to attenuate. Ideally it could reach 1000 and all the fermentables would have been converted into alcohol.

A second listing is of those Yorkshire breweries, mainly small ones, whose beers are not included in this guide.

In the 1990 "Good Beer Guide" published by CAMRA, which covers 5000 pubs in the whole of Britain, 50 beers were selected as Beers of the Year. Of these 10 are available in pubs in this guide and are indicated below (***). They do not represent my choice, as you will see, but they are all worth trying and will no doubt provoke conversation. As I have already implied, choice is a subjective issue.

BASS of Burton-on-Trent and Tadcaster

DRAUGHT BASS (1044) from Burton is not the beer it was but still well respected and worth seeking out. BASS MILD XXXX and BASS LIGHT 5 STAR (both 1031) and SPECIAL BITTER (1036) are from Tadcaster and have no great characteristics but all make for easy drinking.

BATEMAN of Wainfleet

Only the XXXB (1048) is on regular sale. This is an excellent premium beer with a wonderful aftertaste. Their other beers, particularly the XB, a fine bitter of 1036 OG can often be found as guest beers in the free trade.

BIG END of Harrogate

A small free trade brewer that started in 1988. Two beers: PISTON BITTER (1038) (also known as Yorkshire Rose Ale for the prudes) is a pleasant beer and OLD LUBRICATION (1042) has similarities in taste but is darker and richer.

CAMERON of Hartlepool

Now part of the Brent Walker empire but still brewing some good ale including their TRADITIONAL BITTER (1036) a hoppy quaffing bitter and two standards for their well established STRONGARM at 1040 and PREMIUM at 1045. Both are full beers with a strong malt influence.

CLARK of Wakefield

They started brewing again in 1982 after a long lay-off and have created a lengthy portfolio of brews of which TRADITIONAL BITTER (1038), a smooth hoppy beer and the rich and powerful HAMMERHEAD (1056) stand out. Their others are

GSB at 1036, and BURGLAR BILL and WAKEFIELD ALE both at 1044 and of similar origins.

COURAGE of Bristol

DIRECTORS (1046) can be found in several John Smith's pubs. It has good deal of character created by the balance of malt and hops.

CROPTON of Cropton near Pickering

Started brewing in 1984 for the New Inn (qv) but has now expanded. The TWO PINTS (1038) and SPECIAL STRONG BITTER (1058) have a distinct strain of flavour but are vastly different in strengths. All the beers are additive free and brewed with own well water.

EVERARDS of Leicester

OLD ORIGINAL (1050) is often found in Cameron's pubs as part of a trading arrangement. It is a rich beer, disconcertingly stronger than it seems.

HARTLEY of Ulverston

XB (1040) is an excellent beer with a fine aroma and lots of taste. Their other beers include a low gravity bitter which defies its strength.

HOME of Nottingham

Their dark and malty MILD (1036) will be found in Younger's pubs. They also brew a bitter at 1038.

IND COOPE of Burton-on-Trent

ANSELLS BEST BITTER (1037) is an average but not unpleasant beer, whereas ***BURTON ALE (1048) is a classic, very aromatic and full of flavour.

LEES of Middleton Junction

Both of the beers available, GB MILD (1032) and BITTER (1038) are distinctive and with a very good finish to them.

LINFIT of Linthwaite

What can you say of this clutch of beers brewed by Ron Crabtree at his tiny brewery behind the Sair Inn? Enigmatic? Best to try them and make your own mind up: MILD (1032), BITTER (1035), SPECIAL BITTER (1041), ENGLISH GUINEAS

(1041) is a dry stout, OLD ELI (1050), LEADBOILER (1063) and ENOCH'S HAMMER (1080).

MALTON of Malton

Started in 1985, 20 years after the last Malton brewery closed. Now brews four excellent beers with PALE ALE (1034) and DOUBLE CHANCE (1038) both easy drinkers; PICKWICK'S PORTER (1042) is a dry stout and OWD BOB (1055) a dry strong ale.

MARSTON of Burton-on-Trent

A splendid range of beers available in a handful of tied houses in the Dales and widely in the free trade and in Whitbread houses. BURTON BEST BITTER (1036) is a good session beer and MERRIE MONK (1043) an unusual strong mild. PEDIGREE (1043) is their best known and most widely available product and, at its best, is excellent. ***OWD RODGER (1080) is powerful yet goes down easily.

MINERVA of Hull

This is the only one of four Tetley brew pubs to survive and the excellent PILOT'S PRIDE (1040) is the obvious reason why.

MITCHELLS of Lancaster

Two first class brews from a traditional brewery. MILD (1033) is malty and sweet and BITTER (1035) light coloured with a nice mix of flavours. Their ESB (1050) is also good and may be found in the free trade.

MOORHOUSE'S of Burnley

Started brewing in 1979 and now settled in with lots of free trade outlets. The hoppy PREMIER BITTER (1036) goes down well with a good finish and ***PENDLE WITCHES BREW (1050), which deserves its accolade, is full and fruity.

NORTH AND EAST RIDING BREWERS of Scarborough

Another new brewery that is establishing itself. EXB (1040) is brewed to an English style but the others are Scottish with THISTLE BITTER (1040) having all the sweetness and full body of better known brews. The THISTLE MILD (1034) is dark and easy on the palate but the "68" (1050) is nothing special for a premium bitter.

OAK of Birkenhead

Oak started brewing in 1982 entirely for the free trade and seem well established. ***BEST BITTER (1038) is a refreshingly good quaffing ale while OLD OAK (1044) and WOBBLY BOB (1060) are both easy to drink despite their extra strengths. PORTER (1050) isn't a porter but a good strong stout. Also brews TYKE (1041) for West Riding Brewery.

OLD MILL of Snaith

***TRADITIONAL BITTER is a great drink, all you should want in a bitter, good flavour, nose and after-taste. Commenced brewing in 1983 and also does a MILD and premium bitter called BULLION.

ROBINWOOD of Todmorden

Doing very well after less than two years in the business. Supplies nearby Staff of Life pub (qv) and free trade. BEST BITTER (1036) is hoppy and goes down easily, XB (1046) is a fuller and more malty brew and OLD FART (1060) alternatively, XXXX, is a strong dry stout.

RUDDLES of Oakham

Selling mainly alongside Webster's beers as part of the Grand Metropolitan group. BEST BITTER (1037) is a fresh tasting ale and ***COUNTY (1050) for my money is not the beer it used to be. It would not have got my vote.

JOHN SMITH of Tadcaster

After eight years away from traditional brewing they have returned with a vengeance and hand pumps have reappeared in most of their 1450 tied houses. BITTER (1036) is dry and refreshing and the excellent ***MAGNET (1040) is malty with a lovely finish to it.

SAMUEL SMITH of Tadcaster

Yorkshire's biggest independent in the county's oldest brewery. OLD BREWERY BITTER (1039) is full and malty but has dropped in gravity over the years. MUSEUM ALE (1047) is very rich and good for winter evenings.

STOCKS of Doncaster

Yet another new brewery that is doing nicely. BEST BITTER (1037) is hoppy and SELECT (1044) is malty but both go down easily, whereas OLD HORIZONTAL (1054) is dark and subtle.

STONES of Sheffield

Well established Sheffield brewery that is part of the Bass empire. BEST BITTER (1038) is pale and hoppy and easily drinkable.

TAYLOR of Keighley

***LANDLORD (1042) is the prize winner for this small but well–known independent, for its superb distinctive taste. DARK MILD (1033) is GOLDEN BEST (1033) with caramel added; both are malty and drinkable, BEST BITTER (1037) is well hopped and often underrated, and PORTER (1043) is too sweet for its style, whilst RAM TAM (1043) is more like a porter should be.

TETLEY of Leeds

The Yorkshire arm of Allied Breweries with 90 per cent of its pubs selling real ale. BITTER (1035) is a fine beer, smooth and hoppy and MILD (1032) is dark and full of flavour.

THEAKSTON of Masham

Once fiercely independent now part of Scottish and Newcastle. The brewery is traditional and has recently been restored. BEST BITTER (1038) is not as good as it was but still remains a sharp tasting, hoppy beer. XB (1044) is full–bodied and pleasant and OLD PECULIER (1057) a fine dark strong ale came second in the 1989 Champion Beer of Britain but could not make the 50 Beers of the Year list. It would have made mine.

THWAITES of Blackburn

Another independent brewer that sticks to tradition with a light and malty MILD (1031) and a dark, rich and malty BEST MILD (1034). ***BITTER (1036) is a clean beer with a lovely aftertaste.

VAUX of Sunderland

Independent but acquisitive with a tentative attitude to traditional beer. SAMSON (1041) is a sweet beer in the North East style and ***DOUBLE MAXIM (1044) is smoother with a dryer palate. It is a recent addition to their list although it has been a bottled beer for many years.

WARD of Sheffield

A subsidiary of Vaux which also produces Darley beers since its Thorne brewery closed in 1986. DARLEY DARK MILD (1032) is a pleasant fruity beer, DARLEY THORNE BEST BITTER (1037) is drinkable but not the beer they used to brew at Thorne, SHEFFIELD BEST BITTER (1038) is malty and dry and KIRBY ALE (1050) a new innovation, is a rich malty brew.

WEBSTER of Halifax

A Grand Metropolitan company now combined with Wilson's of Manchester whose brewery is closed. CHOICE (1045) is my only choice from this less than average brewery. It has plenty of flavour and hides its strength. GREEN LABEL (1033) is a "best" or light mild of bland appearance and taste, and YORKSHIRE BITTER (1036) would benefit from a renaissance.

WHITBREAD of Castle Eden and Sheffield

A Big Six brewer that takes a less than healthy interest in many smaller companies in which it has a stake. TROPHY (1036) brewed at Sheffield is not the most distinguished beer in the world, whereas in contrast CASTLE EDEN (1040) has many good qualities including plenty of flavour.

YOUNGER of Edinburgh

Their local arm is at Garforth near Leeds and the management display an aggressive attitude in promoting real ale. SCOTCH (1037) is typically Scottish, sweet and pleasant; IPA or occasionally McEWANS 80/- (1042) is also sweet, rather malty and heavy for its gravity. NO 3 (1043) is rich, dark and high quality.

If I were to pick ten beers from those in the above list to be "my 1990 Beers of the Year" and

I must make it clear they are not my ten favourite beers, simply a choice from those available at pubs in this guide, they would be:

Ind Coope Burton Ale
Malton Double Chance
Marston Pedigree
Moorhouse's Premier Bitter
Old Mill Traditional Bitter
John Smith Magnet
Taylor Landlord
Tetley Bitter
Theakston Old Peculier
Thwaites Best Mild

YORKSHIRE BREWERIES WITH NO REGULAR OUTLETS IN THIS GUIDE

ALE HOUSE of Leeds

Above an off licensed shop specialising in traditional beer. Started as a cooperative in 1979 by ten CAMRA members. Brews four regular beers for the shop and occasionally for the free trade.

FOX & NEWT of Leeds

A Whitbread home-brew house that uses malt extract. There are four regular beers and some specials.

FRANKLINS of Harrogate

Set up in 1980 by Sean Franklin and now owned by CAMRA stalwart Tommy Thomas. Only one brew, a BITTER of 1038 OG, with a flowery nose and an aromatic flavour. Serves the free trade.

FROG & PARROT of Sheffield

Another Whitbread home-brew pub, again using malt extract. A long series of beers including one, ROGER AND OUT (1125) which claims to be the strongest beer in the world in alcoholic terms.

MARSTON MOOR of Kirk Hammerton

Started in 1984 by brewing for the Crown Inn where it is based. Now serves the free trade as well with its two regular beers.

SELBY of Selby

Resumed brewing in 1972 after a long lay-off. Off licensed shop in Selby and free trade take its two beers which are in draught form and in bottles.

TROUGH of Idle

Established in 1981 and now has eight tied houses and extensive free trade. Up to recently used malt extract but now has switched to full mashing. Presently producing three beers.

WHITBY'S OWN of Whitby

Started brewing in 1984 and despite some good beer finds it difficult to sell in its home town. Four beers are produced for widespread free trade.

BEVERLEY
Rose & Crown

North Bar Without

- lunchtime and evening
- tables in car park
- for lunchtime meals
- **Ward Darley Dark Mild, Darley Thorne Best Bitter, Sheffield Best Bitter, Kirby Ale; Taylor Landlord; guest beers**
- Beverley

Blue and white buses from the East Yorkshire company used to run between Hull and York and to negotiate the North Bar in Beverley double-deckers were fitted out with specially shaped and rather odd pointed roofs. The memory remains amongst many of the regulars of the Rose and Crown who would sit and watch them pass whilst considering whether to try another pint.

This is the quintessential mock Tudor pub, knocked about a bit inside, but retaining the higgledy piggledy quality that identifies a good house from the ruck. It was the last pub in Beverley to have a "Gentlemen Only" bar where seats were identified and woebetide any stranger who sat in the seat of Herbert or Horace or, indeed, entered the room. But all that has gone and the present place has a friendly atmosphere and a cosmopolitan clientele made to some extent by its location close to the wide open Westwood and the town's racecourse.

Royal Standard (Dolly's)

North Bar Within

- **Ward Darley Dark Mild; Darley Thorne Best Bitter**
- Beverley

This tiny pub is known to all as Dolly's although strictly speaking the name relates just to the back bar where Mrs Dolly Wild presided for more than 30 years. Three generations of the Wild family ran the pub for 100 years until Ken retired in late 1989. But the pub dates back to the seventeenth century although it was refronted in the early eighteenth and in its time its has been called The Boot Hotel and The Turf Hotel. The latter title gives some explanation of its long association with the racing game and behind were stables used until recently by trainers based in the town.

The Royal Standard nestles under the North Bar to the pleasant town of Beverley and stands close to the historic Beverley Arms and St Mary's church. The gem is the front bar which is where the locals gather but overall the pub is basic in its decor and facilities. Therein lies its attraction.

White Horse Inn (Nellie's)

Hengate (next to Bus Station)

- lunchtime and evening
- yard
- lunchtime
- **Samuel Smith Old Brewery Bitter, Museum Ale**
- Beverley

Time seems to have stood still at the White Horse Inn which is better known to most local, and many other, folk as "Nellie's" after a former landlady, the formidable Nellie Collinson. She held court here for almost 50 years catering most of that time for men only and displaying her innate ability to cope with them. Nellie's was, and to some extent remains, an institution. Miss Collinson (she would never have allowed a Ms) ran it her way. There was no bar and drinks were served from a marble topped table. If the room

filled up then customers overflowed into two tiny kitchens. She had a live-in lover known to all as "Suitcase Johnny" because of the number of times he and his possessions were slung out by Nellie after one of their many arguments. But her name is remembered with affection by her former regulars.

The pub has changed a little and now sports a bar and other rooms have been opened up. But its general air of tattiness has thankfully been retained along with its rocking horse sign, coal fires, stone-flagged floors, Victorian prints, huge mirrors and gas lighting. When the Samuel Smith brewery bought the pub in 1976 they discovered that leaks to the gas pipes in the cellar had been mended with chewing gum and there were candles stumps down there as well. Other concessions to modernity include a restaurant and a room made available to families at lunchtimes, but it still remains "Nellie's'.

BRIDLINGTON

Hilderthorpe

Tel: (0262) 672205
Hilderthorpe Road

- ✕ lunchtime and evening (Thu to Sat)
- ☺
- Bass Mild XXXX, Draught Bass; Stones Best Bitter
- ⇌ Bridlington

Bridlington is the archetypal Yorkshire seaside resort, smaller than Scarborough, bigger than Filey, easier to get to than Whitby and with more going on than Hornsea. It has boarding houses, candy floss, summer shows, penny arcades and a harbour where they boil crabs for you to take home to the industrial West Riding. It is also a working fishing port and the Hilderthorpe takes its atmosphere from the harbour and has many fisherfolk amongst its regulars. Tides often determine its busyness quotient.

It is a thriving pub, popular with all ages including children who are made welcome. There is a basic design in the Bass seaside style – functional, comfortable and a nautical theme to the bric-a-brac. The separate dining room, which is generally only open in summer, is well used.

FLAMBOROUGH
Royal Dog & Duck

Dog and Duck Square

✕ lunchtime and evening (not Sun)

❀

☺

🍺 **Draught Bass; Stones Best Bitter**

The village of Flamborough is one mile inland from the splendid cliff scenery and bird watching territory of Flamborough Head, yet it still maintains itself as a fishing village. The Royal Dog and Duck, which is more than 300 years old, takes its name from a barbaric pastime in which tethered ducks were attacked by spaniels. There are several Dog and Duck pubs in Yorkshire and the sport received royal approbation but the "Royal" tag at Flamborough came after a visit in 1900 by Prince Louis of Battenberg, many years after the activity was made illegal.

This is a vast and impressive pub with original beams taken from the spars and masts of an old sailing ship. Children are well catered for here with a family room and an attractive outdoor area, part of which is covered. There are two main rooms, comfortable and with quiet corners. A separate eating area provides reasonably priced food with an emphasis on local produce from the sea.

FLIXTON
Foxhounds Inn

Tel: (0723) 890301
On A1039, seven miles west of Filey

✕ lunchtime and evening

☺

🍺 **Theakston Best Bitter; Younger Scotch, No 3**

From high up on the wolds above Flixton village is one of the best views along the Yorkshire coast, stretching from Scarborough castle to Filey Brig. It is a fine backdrop too for the Foxhounds which presents its long, low attractive frontage to the Filey road. The emphasis here is on food with a separate dining room and a choice of other bars and on summer Saturdays it pays to book in advance. The food is imaginative with good fish dishes and some excellent local meat on the menu. Decor here is pleasant with old beams, open fires and comfortable seating.

HEDON
Shakespeare Inn

9 Baxtergate (off A1033)

12 noon to 7 pm Mon to Sat and Sun lunchtime

seats and tables in car park

Ward Darley Dark Mild, Darley Thorne Best Bitter, Sheffield Best Bitter, Kirby Ale; Vaux Bitter, Samson

Hedon was once the busiest port on the Humber and one of England's smallest and oldest boroughs with a charter dating back to 1348. In Parliamentary terms it was a "rotten" borough returning two members to the House of Commons although most of its small electorate lived elsewhere. Treating – the buying of drinks and meals to secure votes at election times – was rife and vast sums of money were spent to secure votes for Sir Charles Saunders the local MP after whom the pub was first named. Today, as landlord Alex Craig will tell you, the Shakespeare is eminently respectable and accepting drinks implies no concessions.

This one-roomed cosy and friendly old pub is a gem providing first-class ale and excellent food. Susan Craig takes a pride in the freshness and quality of her produce and on Friday and Saturday lunchtimes the haddock comes straight from Hull docks. Other treats include local gammon with free range eggs and jam roly poly. Alex is a CAMRA stalwart and his collection of 3000 beermats decorates the ceiling. The pub was joint winner of the Yorkshire CAMRA pub of the year contest in 1988.

HOWDEN
Barnes Wallis

Station Road

Old Mill Traditional Bitter; Tetley Bitter; guest beers

Howden

A Victorian pub that was built for the railway but which, about four years ago, took a new name to celebrate Howden's most famous son, Barnes Wallis the aviation engineer. There is memorabilia aplenty in the bar. Talk to Bill Robinson, the pub's most enduring regular who first drank here before the Great War and remembers all with great clarity.

The landlord, John Rowan, is an expansive character, who doesn't suffer fools gladly. Asking for lager with two shots of lime will command a sharp response, and ordering a port and lemon, when John sells vintages at around £2 a glass, is akin to treason. He is dedicated to traditional beer and he also stocks an excellent range of bottled beers from Belgium. Music is of the landlord's choice but he welcomes your contributions, particularly on Sunday lunchtimes when it is strictly classical. The Hull branch of CAMRA made it their pub of the year in 1988 and it is easy to see the reason why.

HULL
George

Land of Green Ginger

✕ lunchtime and evening

Bass Mild XXXX, Draught Bass; Stones Best Bitter

The George is the oldest continually licensed pub in Hull and dates from 1449. It was once much larger than it is today but one of its older fascinations still remains – a spyhole through which the porter could watch for the arrival of coaches and keep out undesirables. It is the smallest window in Hull.

Just one large room remains which is sensibly furnished to fit in with the original beams and latticed windows. It always seems busy particularly during the week when the business community take advantage of the first class bar meals – nothing special, just good value. The George also has a restaurant.

Minerva

Nelson Street (opposite Corporation Pier)
Open all day in summer

✕ lunchtime and evening until 8 pm

at lunchtime

Minerva Pilots Pride; Tetley Mild, Bitter

At one time the staff here were required to speak both French and German as the hotel serviced trade from the continental boats that moored at the pier close by. That requirement apart, little else has changed since those early Victorian days except that a four-seater snug was once a ladies' toilet and the place has been carefully renovated. This is a splendid pub, a rambling sort of place with loads of atmosphere and a comfortable, warm feeling about it. Several rooms spread themselves around a central servery and from the smaller lounge are some exceptional views across the Humber.

The river pilots' base is nearby and it was from this that the home brewed ale took its name when a brewery opened here a few years ago – it can be viewed from the street. The reputation for food has spread wide and queues form on Sundays for the excellent lunches. Look around the area and recognise what a good job has been made of rejuvenating it and how well the Minerva fits into it, so it comes as no surprise that it has won a Civic Trust award and a CAMRA Pub Preservation award.

Old Black Boy

150 High Street

Tetley Mild and Bitter

Two hundred years ago there were 50 pubs in High Street, now, there is just this one. It was built in the early fourteenth century and has a fascinating history. Two tunnels led from it – one built during the civil war to the church, the

other to the riverside was used by smugglers. And it is haunted by a friendly and well–dressed man wearing a top hat and white pantaloons. In its time it has had many lives. It started as a private house then became a corn merchants, for a time it was a brothel and later a coffee shop. A tobacconist gave the place its present name when he used an young African as a doorboy and advertising gimmick. A carved fireplace with the Black Boy motif is in the front smoke room. It became a public house in 1775.

The back bar is a source of interest with a collection of prints and some attractive lights hung in clusters. The smoke room with hatch service has some beautiful leaded lights. Essentially this is a drinkers' pub occasionally enhanced by some good folk music.

Old Blue Bell

Market Place

- ✕ lunchtime
- yard
- **Samuel Smith Old Brewery Bitter; Museum Ale**

This fine unspolit old pub which has recently been sensitively refurbished can be found down an alleyway close to the city's market hall. There are three rooms downstairs including a most comfortable and popular snug. David Fletcher, the landlord, is proud of his seasonal floral displays which have won prizes. It is an attractive place, full of character and worth seeking out. The speciality in the lunch menu is Yorkshire pudding, correctly served and not messed about. Upstairs is a music room where on Sundays the long established local folk group – "Folk Union One" – perform.

Olde White Hart

Tel: (0482) 26363
Silver Street

- ✕ lunchtime
- yard
- **Younger IPA, No 3**

It was here in 1642 that the Governor of Hull, Sir John Hotham, took the decision to refuse King Charles I entry to the city by barring the gates against him and thus precipitating the civil war. The carefully preserved "plotting parlour" remains – it is panelled with some excellent carvings and is now a restaurant.

The Olde White Hart can be found up an alleyway in the commercial quarter of the old town, tucked away in an attractive courtyard. Inside some medieval timbering and stained glass remain as well as two enormous sit-in fireplaces and the whole picture is one of a place that has remained unaltered for many years. Atmosphere oozes from it. An elegant staircase leads to the restaurant. They do a very good hot beef sandwich here amongst other things and Sunday lunch is worth arriving early for.

LANGTOFT
Ship Inn

Tel: (0377) 87243
Front Street (B1249)
closed Mon and Tue lunchtime

- lunchtime and evening (Tue to Sun)
-
-
- **Cameron Traditional Bitter; Younger Scotch**

The parish church of St Peter has thirteenth century origins to attest to the age of the village and the Ship sits happily with it in the heart of the community. This quaint local is highly recommended for its comfort, welcome, good ale and excellent food. The small bar is full of character with low beams, an open fire, dark solid furniture and old photographs. The other room is lighter, more open, with lots of brass, a dart board and good conversation. There is a separate restaurant and four en-suite bedrooms

RUDSTON
Bosville Arms

Tel: (0262) 82259
High Street (B1253)

- lunchtime
- in car park
- small room
- **Bass Mild XXXX; Stones Best Bitter**

The Roodstone in All Saints churchyard at more than 25 feet high is the largest standing stone in the country and predates the village, which takes its name, by several centuries even though Rudston is one of the oldest settlements in the wolds. It is almost certainly bronze age and is likely to retain its secret purpose from us and must have been manhandled here from the nearest outcrop of gritstone some ten miles away. The village also has evidence of Roman and Danish influences and the church is Norman in origin. Winifred Holtby, the novelist, is buried here.

The Bosville Arms fronts on to the main road and displays a rather staid exterior but this belies a warm and welcoming place, essentially one room for the children's room on the left is just that. In winter, roaring fires; in summer, muted sunshine. But there is an autumal feel all the year round from the russet decor of the comfortable furnishings. The name is from a local family and a splendid Victorian monument to one of them can be found in the church. A no-nonsense pub where beer and conversation hold sway.

RYHILL
Crooked Billet

Pitt Lane (off A1033)
Closed Tue and Thu lunchtime

✕ lunchtime (except Tue and Thu) and evening

Tetley Mild, Bitter

The Crooked Billet is an attractive white-fronted seventeenth-century inn built in the cottage style, and it fits well in this pleasant Holderness village. It has an old world feel about it and is relatively unspoilt. This was an area for smugglers and the pub was a haunt of theirs. What are now the toilets and part of the lounge was once the village slaughterhouse. Meals are available at all times the pub is open, there are coal fires and access for wheelchairs is easy.

SKERNE
Eagle

Wansford Road, two miles south of Great Driffield

tables in car park

Cameron Traditional Bitter

Driffield 2 miles

Unspoilt country pubs like this are rare. Design a mould for the perfect traditional rural inn and this is what you would come up with. It is unpretentious, with a friendly, warm and welcoming atmosphere and determined to keep it that way. The excellent beer is served from a mezzanine cellar using rare Victorian cash register type beer pumps. Highly recommended. The parish church of St Leonard is worth a visit to see the unusual collection of upright monuments.

SLEDMERE
Triton Inn

Tel: (0377) 86644
At junction of B1252 and B1253

✕ lunchtime and evening

patio

front hall

Younger Scotch

The brick walls of this estate village appear to be turned against the casual visitor but, in fact, Sledmere is a handsome place and there is a welcome at Sledmere House and at the Triton Inn. Sledmere, which has been in the hands of the Sykes family for more than two centuries, is one of nation's great estates and the house is magnificent with work by Capability Brown, Joseph Rose, Chippendale, Sheraton and others. This is horse-breeding territory and of the two monuments in the village one commemorates the Waggoners company of local men and horses who fought in the Great War.

Equine heroes are the theme of the Triton although it takes its name from either an aquatic god – half man, half fish – or one of many ships called this. The bar is a solid place but comfortable and welcoming and the rambling nature of the place gives lots of interest. There is a separate restaurant for which bookings are almost essential and nine letting bedrooms.

Black ancient
wood decor in
Ye Olde White Harte

SUTTON UPON DERWENT
St Vincents Arms

Tel: (0904) 85349
On B1228 eight miles south-east of York

✕ lunchtime and evening

John Smith Bitter; guest beers

The 300 year-old St Vincent Arms took its present name after the first viscount, Admiral Sir John Jarvis, defeated the French at Cape St Vincent in 1801 and was enobled. It was originally two cottages and when it was rebuilt and extended, timbers from one of the admiral's men o' war were used and can be seen today. Reaching the village from York is a pleasant experience taking the traveller through Elvington and across the narrow stone bridge over the Derwent – one of Yorkshire's unsung rivers – and close to Sutton lock.

The pub stands out in a village that is full of attractions including a church with many Norman traces. There are several rooms with the panelled bar at the front particularly outstanding. It has high backed settles, a bow window seat and a coal fire. Other rooms include a restaurant for which it is advisable to book at weekends, and a games room. Children are welcome and there is a large garden. Food ranges from simple sandwiches to elaborate dishes like fillet steak with oyster sauce.

WEAVERTHORPE
Star Inn

Tel: (094 43) 273
On unclassified road midway between Malton and Bridlington

✕ lunchtime and evening

Theakston Best Bitter, XB, Old Peculier

Visit Weaverthorpe, an attractive open wolds village, for its splendid early Norman church with a Saxon sundial and its comfortable two-bar, centre of the village pub. The lounge is relaxing and essentially the visitors' room while the bar is more functional with traditional pub games and a pool area leading off, and popular with all comers. Food is well cooked and reasonably priced and bed and breakfast is available at exceptionally low prices.

O Yorkshire Yorkshire: Thy Ale is so strong,
That it will kill us all if we stay long:
So they agreed a Journey for to make
Into the South, some Respit there to take.
The Praise of Yorkshire Ale...George Meriton

AMPLEFORTH
White Horse Inn

Tel: (043 93) 378
West End

- lunchtime and evening
- in snug
- **Tetley Bitter; Theakston XB**

The Roman Catholic public school is about one mile along the road in this linear village so the White Horse Inn attracts parents, priests and pupils as well local folk and plenty of visitors – truly a cosmopolitan pub for even the landlord, Denis Mackeen, comes from "darn sarf". It dates from the seventeenth century and has been an inn since at least the middle of the eighteenth. It has a stone front with an attractive pantile roof and was formerly owned by Roses of Malton, a brewery with a fine reputation for quality and service which seems to have continued here.

The snug to the right has a splendid wood burning stove, almost continental in style, and is just the place to gather in the depths of winter. Opening off here is a pool room, soon to be made into a separate restaurant. To the left is the bar with a darts area, furnished with wood settles and an open fire. Bar meals are, for the moment, basic but plentiful on the plate; and breakfasts, I am told, are excellent for there are three rooms available for overnight stayers. Kids and dogs are welcome if controlled. The pub is an excellent starting point for several walks in the area.

BELLERBY
Cross Keys

Tel: (0969) 22256
on A6108

- lunchtime and evening
- **Marston Burton Best Bitter, Pedigree**

Ron Hartley is an unassuming sort of chap and may be surprised to find his village pub on the road from Leyburn to Richmond featuring in this guide. It has an uninspiring facade which hides the simple yet welcoming interior of a wonderful, traditional Dales pub. The rooms are comfortable, warm and contrasting with open fires, good conversation and a feeling of well–being no matter how long you have been here. I like the place and often feel like taking advantage of the accommodation available. The food is good and plain; just like the pub, no frills. Visitors might care to take along a key ring to hang on the beams in Ron's collection.

BROTTON
Green Tree

High Street

Cameron Strongarm

You can play chess in this street-corner local with its several rooms, coal fires, easy access for wheelchairs, a garden for children and the tag of the "finest pub in east Cleveland" from the local branch of CAMRA. It is stone-built, completely unspoilt and its atmosphere is friendly. There are no meals but sandwiches are freshly made and the beer is well kept. What more can you ask?

CLOUGHTON
Blacksmith's Arms Inn

Tel: (0723) 870244
High Street (A171 four miles north of Scarborough)

✕ lunchtime and evening

Bass Special Bitter

Cloughton is a pleasant village close to the cliffs and a suitable start point for exploring the North York Moors. The Blacksmith's Arms is traditionally sited opposite the parish church and next to a working smithy from which it takes its name – I wonder how many such pubs, or should I say how many such smithies remain? The stone exterior with its mullioned windows is usually decked with flowers in summer.

Inside the two bars are perfect complements. The front lounge has subdued lighting, low beams, comfortable seating and an open fire. It is the perfect place to relax. The bar is brighter and often boisterous; a social centre for local organisations including cricketers, golfers and the local marrow growing society – a serious business in these parts. This room has cricketing memorabilia and examples of the blacksmith's art. There is a small pool room, a separate dining room and seven letting bedrooms.

"steady!"

COXWOLD
Fauconburg Arms

Tel: (034 76) 214
Main Street

- lunchtime (not Mon) in bar and evenings (not Sun and Mon) in restaurant
- tables at front
- entrance hall
-
- **Tetley Bitter; Theakston Best Bitter, XB**

Coxwold is one of the best looking villages in the North Riding, spoilt only by the amount of heavy traffic rolling through caused by the county council's efforts to make it avoid the nearby one in five Sutton Bank. However, a view up the main street on a sunny summer morning makes it worth getting up early. Broad green swards flank the road to show off some delightful houses and holding sentry at the top is the fifteenth-century church of St Michael with its unusual octagonal tower and the picturesque seventeenth century Fauconburg Arms.

This well appointed inn is long and low with a portico that leads to an entrance hall that is popular with families, particularly at weekends. To the left is the splendid dining room where the pretension of the menu is overcome by the excellent food and reasonably priced wine list. The lounge bar overlooks the main street and its two levels give it interest apart from its good furniture – spindle-backed chairs, long free-standing settles and a sedan chair. The Oak Room at the back, where the locals gather, commands splendid views to the Hambledon Hills. There are four letting bedrooms.

Lawrence Sterne, author of "Tristram Shandy", which many folk talk about but which very few have read, was the vicar here in the 1760s – whether he drank at the Fauconberg is not recorded but his diaries do say that he enjoyed life here and it is easy to understand why.

CROPTON
New Inn

Tel: (075) 15330
Off A170 OS 755889

- lunchtime and evening
-
-
- **Cropton Two Pints, Special Strong Bitter; Tetley Mild, Bitter**

This stone-built imposing pub looks well in the spaciousness of Cropton. The village, on the edge of Cropton forest and at the foot of Rosedale, is interesting with a Victorian church and the remains of a motte and bailey castle. The New Inn has a large garden and a Caravan Club site is next door. It has been updated but is none the worse for that. A single bar serves a pleasant lounge, a family room, a pool room and a restaurant. The food is excellent but none too cheap.

Brewing started in the stone cellar of the New Inn in 1984 originally for the pub alone but with expansion this has now developed into the local free trade and the beers seem to be a must at most CAMRA beer festivals. The distinctive flavour comes from lack of additives and full mashing with its own well water.

DALEHOUSE
Fox & Hounds

Just south of A174 near Staithes

✕ lunchtime and evening

Cameron Strongarm Premium; Tetley Bitter

Dalehouse is the last hamlet in North Yorkshire before you reach that mongrel of a county called Cleveland. The Fox and Hounds is the last building because Roxby Beck which traces the boundary runs around the back of the pub. It is rurally secluded at the base of a small hill in delightful woods and contrasts with the more maritime pleasures of its close neighbour Staithes where Captain James Cook served his

A swift half

apprenticeship. The landlord, also James Cook, is no relation!

The pub is a listed building and has been well cared for both inside and out. Children are welcome and a room is available for them and there are two outside drinking areas – a garden at the rear and a space at the front. Meals are available at lunchtime and in the evening and you can stay overnight in one of the two attached cottages. There are folk music sessions on Mondays.

EGTON BRIDGE
Horseshoe Hotel

Tel: (0947) 85245
Seven and a half miles west of Whitby off A171

- ✕ lunchtime and evening
- **Tetley Bitter; Theakston Best Bitter, XB, Old Peculier**
- Egton Bridge

Idyllic is the only word to describe the setting of this pub in this gem of a village in mid-Eskdale. And that takes nothing away from the attractive eighteenth-century house in its own grounds by the river. It may well take its name from the implements in a game of quoits which is a popular sport in Eskdale. It is similar to the American game of tossing horseshoes but quoits are rings of steel thrown to a hob in a bed of clay.

There has been a gooseberry show in Egton Bridge every August since 1800. It was also the home of Father Nicholas Postgate, the last of the English martyrs who was hanged at York in 1679. The Postgate near the railway station is built on the site of the priest's house.

The Horseshoe, which has a separate restaurant, serves excellent food and has vegetarian meals and a menu for children who are made welcome. The facilities are excellent including a delightfully furnished quiet room, access for disabled people, log fires and pub games. Bed and breakfast is available but is rather pricey.

GLAISDALE
Anglers Rest

Tel: (0947) 87261
Ten miles west of Whitby, south of A171

- ✕ lunchtime and evening
- ⚘
- ⛿
- Tetley Bitter; Theakston Best Bitter, Old Peculier
- ⇌ Glaisdale

This is a pub with a name that explains exactly what its purpose is. For here fishermen can brag about their latest catch without it making a bit of difference to their fellow drinkers or to the locals who have heard and done it all before. It is also a rest for cyclists and walkers but the anglers got there first and the inn has fishing rights for salmon and trout on Glaisdale Beck. But it was not always thus for it started life as Carr End Farm and turned alehouse to serve the local, now defunct iron industry, appropriately called at that time the Three Blast Furnaces.

The facilities here are splendid and are enhanced by stunning views down Glaisdale and the Esk valley where, when not resting, the anglers will be casting their bread upon the waters. The catering provides for children with their own menu and for vegetarians. For the overnight guests there are two rooms suitable for families and a double. Coal fires keep the place snug in winter. The river and the railway station are less than half a mile away and within the village there is room for campers and caravanners.

GOLDSBOROUGH
Fox & Hounds

Off A174, five miles north west of Whitby

- ⚘
- Tetley Bitter

A visit to this pub is worthwhile if only for the views from the back parlour – the sea and the coast across to Whitby are spread out before you. The situation is perfect for this is (in my view) the finest stretch of coastline in Yorkshire. The Fox and Hounds seems to be part of a farm and it is likely that it started life as this in the late eighteenth century. Onion growing is one of the delights on offer here.

Your choice of drinking areas in this simple and welcoming pub are two small rooms on either side of the passage bar. It is delightfully unaffected and old fashioned with only one draught beer on offer along with some good value and straightforward food. Coal fires are a winter attraction and for the summer there is the garden which houses a quoits pitch, a game that is taken seriously in these parts. Children are made welcome.

GREAT BROUGHTON
Wainstones Hotel

Tel: (0642) 712268
High Street
Two miles south east of Stokesley on B1257

✕	lunchtime and evening
	Draught Bass

It started life in 1725 as a farmhouse, was not licensed until the mid 1960s and is now a very popular pub and hotel. Great Broughton was the centre of the nineteenth-century jet industry and the evidence is in the nearby defunct mines and the neighbouring Jet Miners Arms. It is a useful base for exploring the Cleveland Hills and the Captain Cook Trail; the Wainstones has plenty of accommodation for that purpose. The hotel, which takes its name from a local rock formation, is set in two acres of its own grounds. It provides bar snacks and meals in all opening hours and there is a separate alcoved restaurant. Vegatarians and children are well catered for. Families are welcome and the garden is a favourite spot during clement weather.

QUOITS

They were playing quoits in Yorkshire as far back as the fourteenth century. Suggestions that this game was brought here from the United States in the form of horseshoe pitching can be dismissed with ignominy. In 1365, Edward III decreed that his subjects should be forbidden "...to meddle in hurling of stones, loggats and *coits...*" We don't hear a lot about stone hurling and loggats these days but quoits is alive and well and living in the North Riding of Yorkshire.

Most quoit pitches are found in the garden or the car park of a pub, and consist of two boxes, one yard by one yard, filled with clay and sunk flush to ground level 11 yards apart. In the middle is the "hob", an iron stake that projects about two inches. Play is in pairs and from one bed to the other with each player throwing two quoits to try and circle the hob for two points or be nearest to it for one point. Quoits are heavy steel rings lovingly cared for and often passed down through families. A game is 21 up if in a league match or competiton or 11 or 15 up otherwise. Teams are usually of eight players with the individual totals added to give a team score. Arthur Taylor in his excellent book "Pub Games" describes the game in more detail including the tactics and some of its history. He also writes of some other games unique to Yorkshire such as Knur and Spell, Nipsy and Billets.

GRISTHORPE
Bull Inn

Off A165 two miles north west of Filey

✕ lunchtime and evening

Younger Scotch, No 3

Having failed to find a pub in Filey that meets the requirements of this guide it is fortunate that within walking distance a satisfactory alternative is available. The Bull at Gristhorpe is an old whitewashed stone building that dominates the village centre and well worth leaving the main coast road to find. Inside, Tardis-like, it appears much larger than first imagined. A central bar serves three attached but disparate areas – the comfortable but busy "lounge"; the quiet "snug"; and the games-oriented "tap room". The restaurant away from the bar completes the picture to give you all that you could want from a village pub.

GUISBOROUGH
Ship

145 Westgate

Draught Bass

Guisborough was the ancient capital of Cleveland in a magnificent setting on strategic crossroads with two roads to the coast, one to Teesside and the other to the Dales. It is a market town of great character although little remains of its medieval priory which was one of the largest in the country.

The Ship fits well into the terraces of the town centre. It was a former coaching inn and it retains a welcoming and cosy atmosphere. There are real fires, pub games, a walled garden and an interesting collection of maritime relics. There is a warning to take care where you sit for many seats are "reserved" for regulars but, having established that, then prepare yourself for a fascinating session of tales of the past even if some of them are a bit tall. There is a limited amount of overnight accomodation available.

Voyager

The Avenue, Hutton Meadows

✕ lunchtime and evening

dining area

Cameron Traditional Bitter, Strongarm, Strongarm Premium

Here is a pub that does quite a lot of things and does all of them well. It is a modern estate pub but imaginatively laid out on three different levels with bar areas and a restaurant. A wide range of meals is available from snacks to meals with several courses, including Sunday lunch. Bar billiards is numbered amongst the games played here and there is a garden to drink in and for children to play in with loads of swings, slides and the like.

There are camping facilities nearby and its situation close to Hutton village makes it convenient for access to Guisborough Moor, Great Ayton, Roseberry Topping and the North York Moors.

HARMBY
Pheasant

On A648 one mile east of Leyburn

Tetley Bitter

Harmby is the gateway to Wensleydale, where good cheese may be found if you know where to go, but beware the bland pasteurised versions, the cheese world's equivalent of keg beer. If they did bread and cheese at the Pheasant it would be with real cheese for this is a real pub. It is popular too for doing well what it sets out to do – selling good beer. Both its rooms are welcoming, with comfortable furniture and coal fires in winter. There is a pleasant garden and a large caravan site just behind the pub. Chauvinists from the West Riding will be delighted at finding this only outlet for Tetley Bitter in this part of the dales.

HAWES
Board Inn

Market Place

✕ lunchtime and evening

Marston Burton Best Bitter, Pedigree

A market town pub in the second highest market town in England. Hawes is eclectic as a rope making, cheese manufacturing and livestock centre on which its tourist trade sits happily. Tuesday is market day when the farmers come to town looking for business, talk and good ale and food. They gravitate to the stone fronted Board Inn. Modernisation has done nothing to spoil this pub, it remains what it was built to be and the straightforward nature of its welcome and service is ideal. Food is wholesome and plentiful with such plate-fillers as steak and kidney pie amongst the favourites.

HIGH LEVEN
Fox Covert

On the A1044, just south of Thornaby

- ✕ lunchtime and evening
- tables in car park
- **Vaux Samson, Double Maxim**

Do not be deceived when looking for the Fox Covert at finding it close to a place on the map called Sober Hall. The inn is alive and well and selling good ale and food. The setting on the crossroads is attractive for this distinctive clutch of whitewashed one time farm buildings that house a comfortable open-plan interior. It is a welcoming pub which at appropriate times has coal fires. There is a wide menu of bar snacks, full meals including Sunday lunches, daily chef's specials and provision for kids and vegetarians.

HUTTON RUDBY
King's Head

36 North Side
Four miles south west of Stokesley, close to A19

- **Cameron Lion Bitter, Strongarm**

The Kings Head is the choice from a 100 per cent real ale village which can be reached by bus from Teesside and Stokesley. The setting is splendid with mature trees lining the main street and village green and a Norman church across the River Leven. This is a country pub where beer is important. There are three cosy rooms, one of which is available to families although food is not sold. The beams are genuine, the fire is real and the welcome is warm. What more can you want?

Authentic horned hare at the White Bear, Masham

MALTON
Crown Hotel (Suddaby's)

Tel: (0653) 692038
12 Wheelgate

✕ lunchtime and evening

Malton Pale Ale, Double Chance, Pickwick Porter, Owd Bob; Tetley Bitter

Malton

Everybody imagines that this is a home-brew pub but, strictly speaking, the two businesses are separate although there is a family connection and they seem to get on well together. The Crown is a well established hotel on the main shopping street of this flourishing market town. It is exactly the sort of place to drop into after a hard half hour in the supermarket or watching the sheep sales. Malton, happily is full of such places, so search this one out – you will not be disappointed.

It has a smart, white-painted frontage and a worthy sign; the whole effect is welcoming. Inside an unpretentious and tidy bar serves a firm local trade but makes visitors most welcome. Food is of the highest quality as you would expect in a farming area and there is a small dining room to the left front of the house. Behind the main bar is a conservatory, tastefully done, where families are welcome and this opens out into a suntrap of a yard. Up the yard are the premises of the Malton Brewing Company, established since 1985. They operate in converted stables which once housed Double Chance, winner of the 1925 Grand National from which their excellent bitter takes its name.

Spotted Cow

Spitalgate

tables at front of pub

Tetley Bitter

Malton

The Spotted Cow has been a pub since 1864 when it opened to serve the new cattle market but, as a building, it is much older. It is listed and is described as "...typical, unpretentious public house building of its date". That the faceless bureaucrats of Whitehall should pen such prose, albeit in their unenthusiastic way, gives hope for traditionalists and the future of the English public house. Its intentions are as obvious as its roots and until the recent changes in the licensing law it was permitted to open all day on Tuesdays and Fridays to serve the needs of those "having business at the market". It was not a law to be interpreted to the letter.

This is a fine pub and one of the few Tetley Heritage Inns to be found in a rural market town. It is full of character and extremely popular. The tap room is always crowded when the market is in session but will empty in a trice if a favoured heifer comes under the auctioneer's hammer. The sturdy tables are well suited to such a room, along with the wooden settles, and there is an open fire and a mirror from the Roses brewery, its former owner. The comfortable back lounge has an attractive tiled fireplace and there is some noteworthy glass in the bar area. Pictures of old Malton decorate the walls throughout. The food is reasonably priced and substantial in helpings as one would expect in such a pub.

MASHAM
White Bear

Brewery Yard (but not near the brewery)

✕ lunchtime

seats at front

Theakston Best Bitter, XB, Old Peculier

Masham – pronounced "Massum" – is the home of Theakston's brewery and its prize-winning Old Peculier beer. It is a splendid market town with a square to compete with the finest and the venue for several interesting events including a massive steam fair each July. The White Bear has just gone through a phase of refurbishment and there is pleasure in seeing how such a job can be done without appearing to alter the place at all. In fact the only differences appear to be some new and badly needed toilets to the back and an extension to the lounge where the toilets used to be.

A long bar across the back of the pub works for both the lounge to the left and the bar to the right. The comfortable lounge is full of interest with a collection of bric-a-brac to no real theme but ranging from a massive stuffed polar bear to dozens of beer bottles. The bar is basic with television for the sports fans and amongst the games on offer are backgammon and chess.

Imaginative food is served with some original specials that live up to the intriguing smells from the kitchen – there is an oriental element to many dishes – and vegetarians and children are well looked after. On Saturday nights there is live music.

MIDDLESBROUGH
Star & Garter

Southfield Road

- ✕ lunchtime (not Sat)
- tables in car park
- **Draught Bass; Stones Best Bitter; Taylor Landlord; Theakston Old Peculier; Younger No 3; guest beers**

This was once a working mens' club and the conversion was so successful that it won an award from CAMRA's pub preservation group. It retains many of its original features to which have been added some interesting pieces from redundant pubs in the area – the fine Victorian bar is a good example. The games areas are unobtrusive and the large L-shaped lounge has its quiet corners. Pricing is an important feature with a good choice of beers,cheaper than the average for the area, and reasonably priced meals including Sunday lunches. With the conversion came the introduction of real ale which started a movement in Middlesbrough to take it from a beer desert to a reasonable drinking area. The Southfield Hotel next door has an interesting range of beers and provides reasonably priced accommodation.

NEWHOLM
Old Beehive Inn

Tel: (0947) 602703
Off A171, two miles west of Whitby

- ✕ lunchtime and evening
-
- most times
-
- **McEwan 80/-; Younger Scotch**

Newholm is a tiny farming village, stone built, independent and standing a reserved two miles from Whitby. The Old Beehive Inn is a gem of vernacular architecture and dates from around the early eighteenth century. It is low slung and colour washed and stands close to a duck pond that has been listed by the Department of the Environment. Its sign is interesting and contains a verse. Its two rooms are full of character with oak beams, comfortable furnishings and some interesting bric-a-brac such as ships in bottles. An upstairs restaurant does a nice line in local seafood. There are some letting bedrooms and families are welcome with one room available to them at most times.

NORTHALLERTON
Fleece

89 High Street

- ✕ lunchtime
- ☺ lunchtime
- **Theakston Best Bitter, Old Peculier**
- ⇌ Northallerton

Northallerton has a reputation for strong ale that these days must be met by Old Peculier from Theakston's brewery at Masham, 20 miles away. But in its heyday of the seventeenth century the beer sold here had magical properties. According to George Meriton in "The Praise of Yorkshire Ale", a bacchanalian tale of a journey to York, it turned dullards into poets and cripples into athletes as well as making wise men dumb and councillors to look like owls.

The Fleece would have known such beer for this is the oldest house in Northallerton with timber framed gables, stone walls and great oak beams. It can be found behind the old town hall and was originally called the Old Golden Lion. When Charles Dickens stayed here he described it as charming and he would not be disappointed today for what alterations have been made have been done sensitively. There are three separate and distinct areas served from the one bar and another room at the back welcomes children at lunchtimes.

OSWALDKIRK
Malt Shovel

Tel: (043 93) 461
Off B1363, four miles south of Helmsley. OS 623790

- ✕ lunchtime and evening
- ❀
- ☺ tap room
- ⛟
- **Samuel Smith Old Brewery Bitter**

Here's a back to front pub for you. The roadside is attractive but lacks character while around the back there is a magnificent facade overlooking splendid gardens including a box-hedge maze and with views over the Howardian Hills. Open fires are a feature of this cheerful inn with a massive one with logs burning gaily, in the entrance hall – tap room they call it – where children are welcome and the scene is set off by an impressive staircase. The choice of other rooms is: left to the smart lounge with plush upholstery and a bay to the garden; or right and up to the bar, all wooden settles and walking sticks – a place to talk.

The Malt Shovel started life as a manor house in the seventeenth century becoming a coaching inn around 1720. The modern traveller is well catered for as there are three rooms to let here and good food is part of its reputation. They aim to use local produce wherever possible including game when available, with vegetarian alternatives and a menu for kids which forms part of a comic. They have a ghost – of a five year old boy who died in 1890; a significant date.

OSMOTHERLEY
Three Tuns

South End

- ✕ lunchtime and evening
-
-
- **McEwan 80/-; Theakston Best Bitter, Old Peculier; Younger Scotch, No 3**

This is a delightful village and the Three Tuns fits well into it with its flower decked stone front and old sign. Osmotherley is the start point for the Lyke Wake Walk, a 40–mile trek across the moors to Ravenscar on the coast, that has to be done in one 24–hour swoop. It is a mysterious practice based on a medieval poem and a badge given for succeeding is in the shape of a coffin. It is just one of the many bits of history which include visits by Catherine of Aragon who built a chapel here and John Wesley who preached from the butter cross on the village green. It was also the start of the drover's road which paralleled the Great North Road but avoided the turnpike charges.

The inside of the seventeenth-century Three Tuns is bigger than one expects. A small square bar serves a lounge and snug at the front and a larger room to the back which has a dining area opening off. Behind the pub is a splendid beer garden. The furnishings are traditional with lots of wooden settles and some fine sturdy tables. The walls hold prints, maps and documents of fascinating variety including the Instrument of Surrender of the German forces in Holland, Denmark and north-west Germany to Field Marshall Montgomery in 1945. Montgomery, a tactician of impulse rather than precision, managed to get the date wrong. There are even prints in the toilets! It has a high reputation for food including some enormous sandwiches and special meals are put on for Christmas and other occasions.

PICKERING
Bay Horse

Tel: (0751) 72526
Market Place

- lunchtime and evening
- **Cameron Traditional Bitter, Strongarm Premium**

There are plenty of attractions in the immediate vicinity of the Bay Horse including a market every Monday at the front of the pub and the southern terminus of the North York Moors steam railway just around the corner. There is an imposing Norman castle too, a lovely medieval parish church and the Beck Isle folk museum. There is plenty to see here and more besides for Pickering is the Gateway to the Moors.

The Bay Horse was once a coaching inn and had its own brewhouse until 1813. Cromwell's officers were billeted here during the civil war and a large hideaway cavity denotes the unsettled nature of their stay. The historic feel remains in the front lounge with beams, wooden pillars and a roaring fire – very atmospheric – and complemented by the rear bar which is rather brash but comfortable and practical. There is a room upstairs called the Room Upstairs which doubles as a restaurant and a function room for private parties. The reasonably priced home cooked food is imaginative and includes a ploughman's lunch with four kinds of cheese.

Having selected the Bay Horse for this guide it is only fair to say that Pickering is bursting with good pubs and a walk around the town can be very beneficial.

PICKHILL
Nags Head

Tel: (0845) 567391
Six miles west of Thirsk, 1 mile east of A1

- lunchtimes and evenings
- **Tetley Bitter; Theakston Best Bitter, XB, Old Peculier; Younger Scotch**

Pickhill needs finding but this backwater of a village is worth the effort. The Nags Head has a fine reputation for food and a recent change of management has made no difference. The restaurant provides substantial helpings of imaginative dishes made from fresh, and where possible, local produce. The menu changes according to whatever is available and may include simply grilled fresh fish from the coast or local rabbit braised with an orange sauce.

But this is a pub, a village inn, with a tap room where traditional pub games like crib, shove ha'penny, table skittles, darts and doms have a place. You can even play chess here amidst the clutter of jugs, brass and whatever and indulge in conversation; a room to feel at home in. The other bar is altogther more upmarket, the sort of place to impress the boss; comfortable and welcoming. There is overnight accommodation available with huge breakfasts to start the next day's excesses on.

REDCAR
Newbigging Hotel

Tel: (0642) 482059
Queen Street

- lunchtime and evening
- Benches outside
- for meals
-
- **Taylor Landlord; Theakston Best Bitter, XB, Old Peculier; Younger No 3; guest beers**
- Redcar

This is a real community pub – a local – with a reputation for much fundraising for charity. It has been done up in an old fashioned style which seems to fit in with its friendly welcoming atmosphere. The fires are real, there is access for the disabled and there are vegetarian dishes on the menu and small portions (at smaller prices) for the kids. Pub games here include shove ha'penny. There is overnight accommodation and camping facilities are nearby.

RICHMOND
Black Lion

Tel: (0748) 3121
Finkle Street

✕ lunchtime and evening

Cameron Strongarm; Everard Old Original

Richmond is probably the best of the small market towns in the county and its setting is difficult to better with its imposing eleventh-century castle guarding the town to one side and overlooking Swaledale to the other. Amongst other presents it brings are a splendid church, a tiny theatre and some interesting shops. The Black Lion, which has origins in the seventeenth century, stands out in a motley collection of pubs.

It is really a small hotel and has 14 bedrooms and a separate restaurant but it identifies as a pub with its ground-floor facilities which include a no smoking lounge on the right of the entrance lobby and a warm and friendly public bar to the left. There is a snug at the back which is panelled and has a coal fire. The bar meals are very good here and are noted for generous portions.

ROBIN HOODS BAY
Dolphin

Tel: (0947) 880337
King Street

✕ lunchtime and evening

Ind Coope Burton Ale; Tetley Bitter

Most of the pubs in Bay Town as it likes to be called have smuggling connections although the best story relates to the Mens Institute which is opposite the Dolphin and in its former life was the Fishermans Arms. The exisemen surprised a gang of smugglers there with several barrels of brandy, arrested them and confiscated the spirit. To be sure they had the right stuff they sampled it, got a taste for it, finished up drunk and the smugglers escaped.

The Dolphin Hotel, occasionally and pretentiously known as Ye Olde Dolphin, is Bay Town's oldest inn and dates from the seventeenth century so it would have known the smugglers. It is a Grade II listed building that boasts two fronts, on High Street and on King Street. It is large and rambling with a family room, several sets of staircases, overnight accommodation and a reputation, as one would expect in such a town, for excellent seafood dishes (including shark) on its menu.

Laurel

Tel: (0947) 880400
Main Street

in snug

Theakston Best Bitter, XB, Old Peculier

Here lives a landlord who has trailed real ale from one end of the county to the other, or very nearly so. Bob Tucker was an early pioneer of the cause at the Oakleigh in Bradford (qv) and he progressed it to the Bay Hotel just a couple of hundred yards below his present hostelry and on to the Laurel. Yet again there are connections with smuggling.

The Laurel is one of the smallest pubs in Yorkshire and the astonishment is that so many people manage to crowd into it of an evening in comparative comfort. Despite its size it manages to provide a snug which doubles as a childrens' room, a small outdoor drinking area and a good selection of ale. The bar, which is original, was carved out of rock and is just one point of interest in the main room which also displays old photographs, prints and brasses. Outside the window boxes and hanging baskets are magnificent in their seasons. This is a locals' local with darts, doms and crib but most welcoming nonetheless. The opportunity to stay overnight is available in a self-catering flat above the bar; an interesting prospect.

ROMALDKIRK
Rose & Crown

Tel: (0833) 50213
Just off B6277

lunchtime and evening

front terrace

hallway and dining room

Theakson Best Bitter, Old Peculier

What a superb setting there is for this former coaching inn with the village green in front and St Romalds church – 'the Cathedral of the Dales" – beside. It is well suited for visiting Teesdale with its dramatic waterfalls such as High Force and Cauldron Snout and the walks of Hamsterley Forest. Barnard Castle and the Bowes Museum are only seven miles away and Cotherstone of the splendid cheese is next door. This northernmost and least explored of the Yorkshire Dales deserves recognition.

The Rose and Crown provides all the essentials

of a good pub and this has been recognised by most reputable guides. The restaurant has high standards and the breakfast bit of "bed and breakfast" is more than adequate. The front bar is decorated to a farming theme with some weird and frightening tools whose uses exercise the mind – "what the devil is that for?" And the furnishings are traditional to match. The back snug has its own thatched bar and more conventional furnishings and both rooms have open fires. The pleasant entrance hall is popular, particularly in summer. There are self-catering cottages behind the pub. Romaldkirk is no longer in Yorkshire but the pub is a hotbed of support for the county cricket club.

SALTBURN
Victoria

Dundas Street

- ✕ lunchtime and evening
- **John Smith Bitter; Theakston Best Bitter, XB, Old Peculier**
- ≹ Saltburn

This was the first true pub in Saltburn, a quaker holiday town built on the cliff top in the mid nineteenth century, where the only licensed premises were hotels. (The Ship Inn on the seafront is a reminder of the original fishing village that never quite took off.) The setting of the town is well thought out with a gorge as Skelton beck reaches the sea, and views over some of the best cliff scenery in Britain including Boulby cliffs, the highest in England at 666 feet. A lift connects the town with the Italian gardens, esplanade, fine sands and pier.

The Victoria was once a warehouse and has been converted with some style. It is lively with a comfortable feel, the sort of place seaside resorts should contain but rarely do. Good food here commands low prices and is available at all times. The disabled are looked after and there is a choice of rooms. Campers and caravanners can find facilities nearby and the railway station is only 25 yards away.

SCARBOROUGH
Highlander Bar, Stresa Hotel

Tel: (0723) 373426
Esplanade, South Cliff

- ✕ lunchtime
- patio
- ☺
- **Tetley Bitter; William Clark Thistle Mild, Thistle Bitter, EXB, No.68; Younger IPA**
- ⇌ Scarborough

This really is the Highlander in terms of origins, beer styles and decor. It is set in the classic Victorian terrace built on the Scarborough's South Cliff in 1842 in a hotel that caters for all types of visitors including those who favour the luxury of a four-poster bed. The views are magnificent taking in the South Bay, the harbour and the castle. The Highlander Bar allows the opportunity to taste a fine range of beers, four of which are from the brewery just behind the hotel, and one of the largest collection of whiskies in the North of England. The Scottish decor complements both the beer style (the Tetley Bitter allows for the odd chauvinist tyke who may visit) and the whisky. The welcome is always warm and the open fire in winter adds to the general feeling of well–being engendered by a session here.

Hole in the Wall

Vernon Road

- ✕ lunchtime
- **Malton Double Chance; Theakston Best Bitter, XB, Old Peculier; guest beers**
- ⇌ Scarborough

Tucked away below the town centre where the old road to the South Cliff ducks down into the Ramsdale Valley, the Hole in the Wall stands within easy reach of all the facilities of the south side of the town including the Spa, museums, the Georgian Crescent and the commercial heart of Scarborough.

This pub contains several different versions of pleasure; whether you are looking for an old alehouse with wooden floors, darts and a piano, or a snug hidden away for lovers and the like, or the comfort of a pleasant bar with good conversation; you will find them all here. There is also a clock that defies being read and walls that are worth reading. Food is good and cheap and the guest beer policy brings interesting selections from all parts of Britain.

Leeds Arms

St Marys Street (Old Town)

Draught Bass

Scarborough

The Leeds Arms, not to be confused with a near neighbour similarly titled, offers a welcome haven from the brashness and bustle of the promenade less than a hundred yards away. In fact the pub is in the middle of a triangle that has the harbour, the Norman castle and St Mary's parish church with its twelfth century origins, as its points. If you can persuade Les Jensen to show you his cellars hewn from solid rock then you are in for a treat and it will give you some idea why his Draught Bass tastes so good.

Much of the pub's ambience comes from things nautical with fishing nets covering the ceiling and an assortment of maritime bric-a-brac in evidence throughout. It is a compact one-bar pub with subdued lighting and quiet background music – a real gem that the discerning drinker should seek out.

Trafalgar Hotel

Tel: (0723) 372054
Trafalgar Street West

✕ lunchtime

Cameron Traditional Bitter, Strongarm

Scarborough

This is a popular local just far enough out of reach of the town centre to give it a relaxed atmosphere. It was built at the time that the Victorian town was expanding when Scarborough was crowned "Queen of the Watering Places". It has a dignified and straightforward facade, delightfully bedecked with flowers in summer, that fits in well with its neighbours. The bar is basic but always busy and the shelf of sporting trophies leaves you in no doubt of the ability of the pub's regulars be it at pool, darts or dominoes. The lounge is comfortable – an ideal meeting place.

SNEATON
Wilson Arms

Tel: (0947) 602552
Just off B1416, two miles south of Whitby

✕ lunchtime and evening

Cameron Strongarm; Tetley Bitter

Ruswarp

Children are welcome in this large pub set in a quiet village way above Whitby. Apart from a room for families there is a garden and a large play area with swings and slides and an inflatable castle. There is a friendly atmosphere all round. The younger set find the place popular but tend to stick to the pool room and the discotheque where no real ale is served.

It started life in the seventeenth century but has been extended recently. There is an interesting collection of militaria and the place is said to be haunted. Meals are available at both lunchtime and evening sessions and there is overnight accommodation.

STAINTON
Stainton Inn

Off B1380, just south of Middlesbrough

✕ lunchtime and evening

Cameron Strongarm, Strongarm Premium; Everard Old Original

Stainton village shows the value of green belt policy by just escaping becoming a suburb of Middlesbrough and is all the more attractive for that. The Stainton Inn in the middle of the village is one of the best eating houses in the area and if you are wanting a meal it may be prudent to ring ahead. If it is just a drink you want then it is still a wise choice.

It is an imposing red-brick Victorian pub that

was extended a couple of years ago into next-door cottages. There is a main bar with a separate and unobtrusive dining area and a garden for outdoor drinking. Vegetarians and children are well looked after in the restaurant where they only use fresh produce. Seafood such as mussels and lobster feature on the daily "specials" board, and roast beef and "Yorkshires" on Sunday lunchtimes drag in crowds from Teesside's urban wastes.

YORKSHIRE PUD

There is an old saying that you can't find good Yorkshire pudding outside Yorkshire. You can try but they are best avoided. But the worst I ever had were in the Royal Station Hotel in York where it appeared on the menu to accompany Boeuf de roti, as "Poudin d'York". I ask you: how could it be any good with that sort of nonsense?

There is no mystique about making them, although I suspect many Yorkshire cooks like to create one. "Only use two-day old milk" says one; "leave the mixture to stand for at least two hours" says another, and there are contradictions – 'Always beat it" or "never beat it". The best advice is to find a method that suits you and stick to it.

I was weaned on the stuff. It was always our starter on Sunday whether roast beef or whatever was to follow, and was always accompanied by lashings of thick beef or sometimes rabbit gravy. Another piece appeared with the main course – we even had it on Christmas Day along with the turkey – and occasionally it was back again covered in syrup for sweet.

So, for the record, here is the family recipe passed down for at least four generations:

To make one large pudding, use a 9" square baking tin well greased with beef dripping taken from the roast. Whisk one egg well and from a half pint of milk add about two tablespoons. To this gradually work in four ounces of plain flour (never self-raising) which has been sieved with a pinch of salt, and then add the rest of the milk. Leave for an hour or two and whisk again. Heat the baking tin in a hot oven (200 degrees C) until the fat smokes blue. Add the mixture and cook for about 30 minutes by which time it will have risen well up the tin, turned golden brown in colour and the edges will be crisp. This deserves better than gravy from a packet, so either use the juices from the roast or make some from shin beef.

The trendy places muscling in these days on its popularity are filling them with all kinds of nonsense including chilli and curry. There is a rightful place for these excellent dishes when they are properly cooked but it is not in a Yorkshire pudding.

STAINTONDALE
Shepherd's Arms

Tel: (0723) 870257
Off A171, seven miles north of Scarborough

- lunchtime and early evening
- Cameron Traditional Bitter

The moors meet the sea at Staintondale and the landscape is suitably impressive despite the apparent isolation of the place. The casual visitor may wonder where the regulars come from after pausing at the doorway to survey the dale with its handful of farms and the coastal panorama to Flamborough Head some 25 miles away and including Scarborough castle and Filey Brigg.

After entering it is however, easy to settle into the calming rural atmosphere of the appropriately named Shepherd's Arms. Its charm lies in the tidy and unspoilt state of the lounge and the bar with speckled sunlight or roaring fires determining the seasons. Conversation is easy here whether it be sporting prowess, the world at large or the antics of a visitor that is the subject – the only thing to remember is not to take yourself too seriously. The quality of the beer may contain the secret of the landlord's other passion – growing weighty marrows. There are three letting bedrooms.

STAMFORD BRIDGE
Three Cups

Tel: (0759) 71396
Stamford Bridge West

- lunchtime and evening
- garden with children's play area
- Stones Best Bitter

This historic village was the scene of the other battle in 1066 after which Harold marched his troops from victory over the Saxons, 250 miles south to defeat by William the Conqueror. Played two, won one, lost one, as the Chelsea (no relation) supporters might have put it. The River Derwent splits the village into two counties and the Three Cups is in North Yorkshire, sited where there has been an inn since 1215.

The pub has been modernised and opened out but a medieval well remains visible through portholes in the bar. Food is important here with snacks and meals available during all sessions. There is a restaurant with an extensive menu including vegetarian dishes. A large outdoor drinking area is most suitable for children being away from traffic and parking is easy. There are two letting bedrooms.

STOKESLEY
Station Hotel

Station Road

- lunchtime and evening (not Sun)
- **Theakston Best Bitter, XB, Old Peculier**

Stokesley is a fine town with the River Leven running its whole back-length. You cross the river towards Kirby to find the Station which was built in 1861 to serve the now defunct rail connection between Battersby and Picton. The front bar is a light and airy place and there is also a quiet snug and a popular function room. Jim Briggs has been the landlord there for many years and his welcome is genuine and enduring.

Excellent bar meals – all home cooked – are available lunchtime and evening every day except Sunday. There are coal fires, facilities for the disabled and pub games including bar skittles. A campsite is nearby. The location is good for Great Ayton and the Captain Cook trail.

THIRSK
Olde Three Tuns

15 Finkle Street

- lunchtime (not Sun)
- small
- **Tetley Bitter**
- Thirsk

This is the oldest pub in Thirsk, a town that has a sufficiency of old pubs, but it is rather special in that the market square is clustered with former coaching houses and the Olde Three Tuns, just off the square in what is known as Old Thirsk, is really a village inn. It is a rambling sort of place with a square bar to serve what is basically one room although the judicious use of existing walls creates several disparate drinking areas. There is an upstairs room where pool is played but which can be used for functions. The atmosphere intrigues and perhaps this is due to the cosmopolitan nature of the drinkers which include locals, visitors and the office crowds at lunchtime. It is a cheerful place. Food is of the "chips with everything" style with generous proportions at reasonable prices. The speciality of the house is giant Yorkshire puddings with various fillings – giant means about the size of a flat cap!

TUNSTALL
Bay Horse

Tel: (0748) 818564
Three miles south west of A1 at Catterick
Closed winter weekday lunchtimes

✕ evening Wed to Sat

Samuel Smith Old Brewery Bitter

Tim Richards combines the job of landlord of this pleasant little roadside pub with that of assistant postmaster of Tunstall. It reflects the fact that running a country pub is not all some folk imagine it to be. The suprising thing is that this eighteenth century pub is still here, for there was once an intention to move it stone by stone to a projected folk museum in York, fortunately it didn't happen.

The simple format of the pub, with a comfortable lounge served by a hatch from the bar in the cheerful tap room, makes it essentially a locals' place. But it is more than that and the welcoming atmosphere is evident. This is a good place to explore from, to the northern dales and the pleasures of towns like Richmond, Thirsk and Northallerton. Three rooms are available to let and there is a dining room to seat 20 to which a complete Yorkshire range adds a good deal of character. There is great enthusiasm for traditional pub games including the local favourite, quoits with the pitch just across the road. A five van caravan site is located behind the pub and a pleasant garden at the side completes an attractive picture.

UGTHORPE
Black Bull

Tel: (0947) 840286
Off A171, six miles west of Whitby

✕ lunchtime and evening

Tetley Bitter; Theakston Best Bitter, XB, Old Peculier

For the adventurous there are several ways of finding Ugthorpe: what you need is a steady nerve and a good map, but whether on two feet, two wheels or four, the journey is worthwhile. The Roman Catholic church should be visited and has some glasswork to designs by Augustus Pugin a man who transferred his christianity into his architecture. There is also a decapitated windmill.

The Black Bull is set in a row of seventeenth-century cottages in the middle of the village. One welcoming trait is the lack of a jukebox and another is the folk nights on Saturdays. Good value food, in which fresh fish plays an important part, is available at lunchtimes and in the early part of the evening sessions which start at 7 pm. There is a spacious tap room, a comfortable snug, a separate dining room where children are welcome and an outside drinking area at the front of the pub has a quoits pitch. Bed and breakfast is available at most reasonable rates but there are only two rooms.

WHITBY
Black Horse

Church Street

lunchtime and early evening

Tetley Bitter

Whitby

This was a pirates' pub, or so I was told. I suspect, more properly, it was and remains, a seafarers' refuge. Not only do they drink here but they are famed and framed on the walls either in the sepiawork of Frank Meadows Sutcliffe whose photographs introduced Whitby to south of Watford, or in the drawings of Stephen Selby an American artist who fell in love with the place in more recent times. (You do a double take somtimes in the tap room when fishermen playing dominoes are watched by images of themselves also playing dominoes.)

The tap room is the heart of the Black Horse and a recent renovation was sensitively done to the satisfaction of the denizens. Another touch by Selby is a carving from a tree stump of his view of the 1861 lifeboat disaster. It is obvious in Whitby that the sea is all around us. There is another carving in the recently extended back room which now offers the privacy of alcoves. Children are allowed in here and in the pool room upstairs at lunchtime and in the early evening.

In coaching days the Black Horse, which is tucked away by the market and the east pier, serviced the runs to Scarborough and York. It is the oldest trading pub in the town and its yard was once the midden of St Hilda's Monastery. When the pub was rebuilt in 1874, bones, shells and domestic waste were found here.

Whitby pub sign

Little Angel

Tel: (0947) 602514
18 Flowergate

- ✕ lunchtime (Sun in summer only)
- **Tetley Bitter**
- Whitby

History plays a big part in the make-up of the Little Angel, perched on a hill above the harbour almost out of the town, as a stone outside shows it to be on the boundary of the parishes of Whitby and Ruswarp. The first building on this site was a brewhouse for a monastery but the present one has its origins in 1823 when it was called the Abbey Inn. At that time it consisted of just the present tap room but later the house next door was bought and the pub extended.

There is a warm feeling about the place, particularly in the lounge with its dark oak panelling and comfortable furniture. A point of interest is a medieval casement window that has been set into a wall. The tap room is a classic, traditional in every way although darts players have been known to complain about the low beams. Home-made steak pie is a favourite on a menu that attracts many visitors in summer.

YARM

Ketton Ox

Tel: (0642) 788311
100 High Street

- ✕ lunchtime and evening Thu to Sun
- ⊕ until early evening
- Vaux Samson, Double Maxim

The Ketton Ox is the oldest pub in Yarm; a former coaching inn that is more than 400 years old. It takes its name from a famous shorthorn bred by Charles Colling of Ketton which weighed 220 stone. There are two rooms on the top floor and one of them was the official cockpit until it the so-called "sport" was declared illegal in 1849. The other then became the unofficial venue and had such facilities as a set of secret stairs to the floor below and a chute down which the cocks were rushed to a shed in the yard.

Today it is a cosy and friendly local with a fine reputation for food with all tastes catered for. Its popularity is such that you are advised to check ahead if contemplating a meal and you must book for Sunday lunches. There is a wide range of food and occasionally gourmet evenings are held. The pub is open-plan but warm and welcoming.

There must be inns in Paradise
   Where nappy ale is sold,
And beef and pickles – even pies
   Such as we've known of old!
      And we will find a parlour there,
      And call for pints for all to share!

Dales in Paradise...A J Brown

ADDINGHAM
Swan

Main Street

✕ lunchtime

Bass Light 5X; Draught Bass; Stones Best Bitter

Entering the Swan is akin to going back in time a century or so. It has other pleasures too as a rare refuge from the modern noise and bustle of Addingham's main street – they have been fighting for a by-pass here since the internal combustion engine was a lad. The atmosphere is unusually peaceful and very friendly. There is a room at each corner of this pub with differing personalities and adherents and a stand-up drinking area which is always popular in the West Riding tradition. A ghost is said to live here and may well be one of the former occupants of a now disused room that was once the village mortuary.

APPLETREEWICK
New Inn

Tel: (075 672) 252
Six miles south east of Grassington, close to B6160

✕ lunchtime

John Smith Bitter; Younger Scotch, No 3; guest beers

For years this claimed to be "Yorkshire's only non-smoking pub". It was in the days of Jack Showers, an amiable eccentric who once threatened to sue me for calling him that. He campaigned against the perils of tobacco after a friend of his died from cancer. The present owners relaxed the ban and installed smoke extractors instead. This four square pub has some of the finest views in the dales and fits well into this straggling village where "Dick Whittington" was born.

It is a welcoming pub with an L-shaped bar serving a pleasant main room with an open fire. There is a separate room across the corridor where children are made welcome and a colourful garden. Bed and breakfast is available with one single and three double rooms. A range of more than 40 bottled beers includes some interesting foreign ones such as trappist brews from Belgium. Food here is hearty, all home cooked, and includes a ploughman's with three different kinds of cheese. Evening meals are available at the nearby Craven Arms.

ARNCLIFFE
Falcon

Tel: (075 677) 205
On unclassified road, three miles from Kilnsey on B6160

- ✕ lunchtime
- ☺ lunchtime
- 🛏
- Younger Scotch

Halfway up Littondale, on the far side of the attractive village green is this unspoilt dales inn where nothing much has altered during the reign of four generations of the Miller family as landlords. It is sited at the beginning of a track to Malham over some of the best looking fells in Yorkshire and the narrow road that mirrors it provides a most exciting drive. Charles Kingsley lived in the village when he wrote "The Water Babies" and Arncliffe has been the refuge of poets, artists, fishermen and walkers over the years, with the Falcon giving succour to all. The pub has four miles of fishing rights on the River Skirfare.

The front of the Falcon, with its two magnificent bay windows, is covered in ivy and gives clues to the pleasures inside. Beer is served from the cask in a small servery which has hatches to two small rooms furnished with settles and heavy tables, and seasonally there are fires. At the back is a conservatory where children are welcome at lunchtimes.

Food is of a simple nature, such as pies and sandwiches, elaborating to baked potatoes and a ploughman's but the quality and value are good. Bed and breakfast is available.

BOROUGHBRIDGE
Three Horseshoes

Tel: (042 332) 2314
Horsefair

- ✕ lunchtime and evening until 8.45 pm
- ☺
- 🛏
- Vaux Samson

A family-run hotel in an ancient town that, happily, has been by-passed by the A1 trunk road. Boroughbridge was attacked by the devil in early Christian days and the evidence remains in the shape of three arrows which are in fact bronze age standing stones of great height and weight in the fields around the town – they form one of Yorkshire's most famous prehistoric monuments. There is more antiquity nearby at Alborough where two fine Roman pavements are preserved.

Boroughbridge was an important coaching station on the Great North Road and a river crossing. The Three Horseshoes has a long history but the present building dates from the thirties and this shows up well. The feel of the place oozes comfort and touches like an unusual tiled fireplace in the lounge, and leaded lights and wood panels in the bar add to the atmosphere and character. It eschews a juke box in favour of a piano. A full range of meals is available. There are 12 letting bedrooms of various sizes, some with bathrooms and all at reasonable rates.

BREARTON
Malt Shovel

Off A61 and B6165, four miles north west of Knaresborough
Closed Mondays

- lunchtime and evening
- paved area behind pub
- **Big End Piston Bitter; Old Mill Traditional Bitter; Theakston Best Bitter, XB; Vaux Samson**

A charming sixteenth century village pub, a little off the beaten track but worth the effort to find. The outside is of white rendered stone and the stone persists inside with some marvellous old beams. The ceilings are low, the windows are tiny and the whole picture is one of tradition. The main lounge houses the bar and some comfortable furnishings with glorious log fires in winter. The smaller room is the games room, used also for eating. The food is high quality, home-cooked and much sought after. Specials on the menu tend to vanish in the early part of the session. There is a specially constructed ramp for wheelchairs from the car park to the back door.

BURLEY-IN-WHARFEDALE
White Horse

Main Street

- **Tetley Mild, Bitter**
- Burley-in-Wharfedale

'Little gem" is a bit overused in guides like this but "little gem" is the only way to describe the White Horse, set in a terrace on Burley's main street. Just railed steps to a door and two windows are all it offers to the streetscene, whitefronted and neat but nothing spectacular. Along the corridor brings you to the bar, with its warm welcome and amazing collection of bric-a-brac. It ranges from a two hundredweight dog grate protecting the coal fire, through assorted brasswork, bottles, jugs, guns and a set of pressure gauges. There are photographs too, of all the pubs there ever were in Burley except the White Horse! Sunshine shows up a pair of windows from former owners Melbourne of Leeds with its famous trade mark of the bowing courtier. They play dominoes in the bar and darts in the miniscule snug that leads off and overlooks the main road.

CHAPEL LE DALE
Hill Inn

Tel: (0468) 41256
On B6265, four miles north east of Ingleton

- ✕ lunchtime and evening
- ❀
- ☺ small room
- ⛟
- ⊕ **John Smith Bitter; Theakston Best Bitter, XB, Old Peculier**

Chapel le Dale at the foot of Ingleborough is the heartland of caving country and a suitable place for tackling the famous three peaks of Yorkshire, although the official starting point is Horton in Ribblesdale. The Hill Inn is the climbers inn but it attracts also walkers – the Pennine Way and the Dales Way are about three miles up the road – and, of course, cavers and potholers. It was built in 1615 and amongst its many visitors have been Robert Southey, J M W Turner and John Buchan.

Substantial meals are served to the energetic and others alike in the dimly-lit large public bar where in their more relaxed moments, climbers have been known to make a circuit of the room without touching the floor. This is an interesting, exciting place with occasional sessions of live music, sometimes arranged, sometimes not. Accommodation is available and there is a camp site nearby. Train buffs may also find pleasure here for the famous Ribblehead viaduct on the Settle and Carlisle line is only a couple of miles away.

CRAY
White Lion

Tel: (075 676) 262
On B6160, just north of Buckden

✕ lunchtime and evening

Moorhouse Premier Bitter; Theakston XB; Younger Scotch

The White Lion takes its name not from heraldic sources but, as a former landlord told me, from the white foam caused by the roaring waterfall nearby. The simple tales are the best ones. There are waterfalls all around with those at Aysgarth and West Burton particularly worth visting. It is the highest inn in Wharfedale and its setting, 1000 foot up on the flank of Buckden Pike, is spectacular yet easy of access on the main road into Bishopdale and Wensleydale. In bygone days it was used by pack-horse traders and drovers taking their cattle from Scotland to the markets of the midlands and south.

The original beamed ceilings and stone-flagged floors of this seventeenth-century building have been retained in the main bar. Walkers are welcome and can be found warming themselves at the open fire. There is some interesting bric-a-brac including farming tools, china plates and the game of ring the bull is famous here and known as "bull "ook". There is a separate small dining room with good plain food including casseroles, ham and eggs, sandwiches and pie and peas. Outdoor drinking, and eating, is popular in the pretty garden or alongside the tumbling stream across the road.

HARROGATE
Hales Bar

1 Crescent Road

✕ lunchtime

Draught Bass; Stones Best Bitter

Harrogate

There is a shabby respectability about Harrogate these days, it has lost some of its gloss. The hotels are not family owned any more and the string quartets have left the tea shops. Perhaps it is because the ladies no longer wear flamboyant hats and the multi-million pound, over-priced conference centre is too dominant. But there is still Hales Bar. The main room here never seems to change, with its gas lighting and mirrors and a respectable sort of comfort with a degree of privacy. Tall brass cigar lighters on the bar give a turn of the century touch and the bar back advertises "Porter" although it is many years since it was served. The alcoves are popular with business dealers and lovers and, at times, happily shared. Lunchtimes are hectic, evenings are more placid, but the atmosphere remains friendly, the service is swift and the food is all you would expect of this sort of established alehouse. The smaller room to the left has been modernised and the television is intrusive; but why leave the main bar?

HETTON
Angel Inn

Tel: (075 673) 263
Just off B6265, four miles south of Grassington

- lunchtime and evening
- pub forecourt
- Taylor Landlord; Theakston Best Bitter, XB, Old Peculier; Younger Scotch

Hetton is a quiet little village handily placed for Wharfedale or to the south, the Embsay steam railway where they serve Selby Fireiron Bitter on handpumps. The Angel is a long-fronted stone building with a choice of rooms including a main lounge with low slung beams and a farmhouse range. This is a comfortable pub but, be warned, it has a great reputation for food and gets very busy, particularly at lunchtime during the summer and on most weekends. But in the evening the quiet cosy alcoves are there for the taking and real fires warm each room. The restaurant meals are not cheap by pub standards but the menu is imaginative and not only is it all home-cooked but they cure and smoke foods here too. The fine range of beers is well kept and complemented by an interesting wine list which includes some bin ends and a number of malt whiskies.

HUBBERHOLME
George

Tel: (075 676) 223
Off B6160, one mile north west of Buckden

- lunchtime and evening separate restaurant
- patio
- family room
- Younger Scotch Bitter, IPA

J B Priestley loved the Dales and this area in particular and whilst he wrote well of several pubs it seemed that the George was his favourite. His ashes are buried in the churchyard across the bridge. The inn, the church and the bridge make up the county's smallest conservation area. The Wharf is still in its birth pangs as it bubbles its way through Hubberholme – named after the Viking King Hubba who settled there. This delightful hamlet is at the foot of one of the highest motor roads in England at more than 1900 feet over Fleet Moss to Hawes.

The George is a mixture of eighteenth and nineteenth-century buildings that in their time have been farmhouse and vicarage and up to recently were owned by the ecclesiastical commissioners with the rent going to the stipend of the vicar. This traditional and unspoilt inn has two stone-flagged rooms and retains some of its original mullioned windows and wooden beams. Food quality is high with home-made soups and pies and well–filled sandwiches. There are five letting bedrooms.

Behind the George is a 16–acre field, known as Poor Pasture, which is let off by auction on the first Monday in each New Year. The ceremony is called the "candle auction" and the "Lords", the Vicar, the churchwardens and the past tenant, go into one room; while the "Commons", the rest of the customers, go into the other and the proceeds go to the old folk of the parish.

ILKLEY
Ilkley Moor Vaults

Stockeld Road

- ✕ lunchtime
- garden
- Taylor Best Bitter, Landlord; Tetley Mild, Bitter
- ⇌ Ilkley

Most people in the town know this pub as "The Taps" from the days when it was the tap room to the Ilkley Moor Hotel which was sadly destroyed by fire in 1968 and only the Taps survived. It is situated in a pleasant leafy part of the town just off the Skipton Road, handily placed for the river and the start of the Dalesway footpath which links to the Lake District. The town, with its fashionable boutiques and dinky little tea shops, is but a short amble away.

According to its sign the Vaults is a free house but actually it is managed by Tetleys who occasionally follow where others have set trends, and allow guest beers into their houses. There is a rural feel about the place with its stone floors and panelled walls and the terrace bar upstairs which, sadly, only opens at weekends.

Wharfe Cottage

Leeds Road

- ✕ lunchtime and evening until 8.30 pm
- garden with play area
- **Ruddles Best Bitter, County; Tetley Bitter; Theakston XB; Webster Choice; guest beers**
- ⇌ Ilkley

A pub that was born out of the real ale revival; it was a couple of terrace-end houses until 1978 when, following a public inquiry at which I gave evidence for the owner, it received planning permission for change of use and subsequently a licence. It has never looked back and the variety and quality of real ale has been paramount. I am also available for masonics, bar mitzvahs and young farmers' dinners.

The owners have done their best to create a genuine Dales atmosphere here with some good stained glass being installed and traditional pub games including shove ha'penny. The menu is extensive with good value, home-cooked dishes including alternatives for vegetarians and small portions for children who have their own play area. A pianist tickles the ivories on Sunday evening. The town centre is quite near – Ilkley, amongst its many pleasures has some good book shops.

KNARESBOROUGH
Mother Shipton Inn

Low Bridge

- ✕ lunchtime and evening
- **Younger Scotch, No 3**
- Knaresborough

Peter Davison, landlord of the Mother Shipton, impressed me when he told me that he didn't pass bottles over the bar but poured out the beer himself. Like me he detests the obnoxious practice of drinking direct from a bottle. Ugh. And a traditional pub like this deserves to, and indeed does get better. It has been settled happily alongside the low bridge over the River Nidd for around 300 years and is next to the entrance to the Long Walk and the Dropping Well. Mother Shipton lore is important to Knaresborough and although she was an ugly old besom, occasionally her prophecies came to something.

This fine stone building is a maze of rooms and passages, alcoves and snugs with a prominence of dark oak panelling and some fine furniture including a seventeenth century table and an interesting chest. A small room to the left of the entrance is available for families. The garden is first class, overlooking the river and with views to the town's famous viaduct. The pub is handy for the castle, the market square and the towns other attractions.

LINTON IN CRAVEN
Fountaine Inn

On B6265, just south of Grassington

- ✕ lunchtime and evening
- **Tetley Bitter; Theakston Best Bitter; Younger Scotch**

This is a delightful village with a Norman church, a Georgian hospital and almshouses and at least five ways in which it is possible to cross the beck: by three bridges, a ford and stepping stones. Charity often leaves its mark by way of commemorative plaques, statues and public buildings, but rarely by a public house. But the village inn remembers Richard Fountaine who endowed the almshouses.

The Fountaine is a splendid seventeenth-century listed building with an unspoilt, low-beamed interior of several rooms. The front bar is comfortable with a large open fireplace and a snug has some interesting high-backed settles.

Ringing the Bull is played here along with other pub games. The food includes specially made sausages containing spices, herbs and walnuts; a vegetarian dish each day, some simple pleasures like sandwiches and sole and salmon when available.

LITTON
Queens Arms

Tel: (075 677) 208
On an unclassified road six miles north west of Kilnsey on B6160

✕ lunchtime and evening

Younger Scotch

Way up Littondale in a beautiful narrow valley is this perfectly preserved pub which dates from the early seventeenth century. There is some exciting motoring around here and the journey over Halton Gill and under the shadow of Pen-y-ghent to Ribblesdale is tremendous. For the active this is fine walking country and the Queens can provide all the facilities needed whatever way you choose to travel.

The main bar is stone-flagged, with stone walls and mullioned windows and a roaring fire warms the place in winter. The family room on the left is full of varnished pine and is carpeted. The food is high class and the quality of the beer has been recognised by Youngers with several awards of excellence. Lunchtime food is substantial with soups and sandwiches and a hot dish or two, slightly more up beat in the evening although nothing pretentious – steaks and the like, good Dales eating. Accommodation is available and the breakfasts are said to be generous.

Stuffed fox at bay in the Ilkley Moor Vaults, page 77

LONG PRESTON
Maypole

Tel: (072 94) 219
Maypole Green (A65)

✕ lunchtime and evening

Hartley XB; Whitbread Castle Eden Ale

Long Preston

This eighteenth century traditonal building with a stuccoed facade faces on to the village green and the maypole from which it takes its name. The lounge bar is comfortable and neatly furnished and has an open log fire in winter. The tap room is spacious where pub games are important if not predominant. There is also a separate dining room. Food is an attraction here with some typical Dales fodder such as ham and eggs, big steaks and roast beef lunches on Sundays. Children and vegetarians are well looked after. Accommodation is available and the pub is conveniently sited for the Malham and Settle districts and close to a station on the Settle and Carlisle railway.

LOWER BENTHAM
Punch Bowl

Tel: (0468) 61344
On B6480

forecourt

Mitchell Mild, Bitter

Bentham

This is the westernmost pub in modern Yorkshire, just 200 yards from the Lancashire boundary and only 17 miles from the Irish Sea at Morecambe. The recently exposed rubble-built sandstone is typical of many of the local houses and farms. There are drip stones on its front and on an adjacent barn, with the initials IW on both, but with dates on them of 1670 and 1708, indicating that it was extended. A mounting stone is still there and inside is a magnificent Victorian engraved glass door panel.

Inside are a comfortable lounge and a public bar that has been extended into the living space and which drops to another level for a pool table area. Accommodation is available here and residents have fishing rights on the River Wenning which flows some 20 yards from the front door.

Sun Dial

Main Street

- ✕ lunchtime and evening (not Mon)
-
-
- **Thwaites Mild, Bitter**
- ⇌ Bentham

The Sun Dial is a pleasant double-fronted building at the junction of the village's main street and the Burton in Lonsdale road. It is built of uncoursed local sandstone and presents a happy picture for the thirsty drinker. For many years this was a Yates and Jackson house until that fine independent Lancaster brewer fell to a takeover in the mid 1980s. However it remains popular and has much to offer. The inside of this eighteenth-century pub was opened out many years ago as is displayed by the irregular shape of the bar. The pub has a bistro, a garden and accommodation is available. The Sun Dial had momentary fame some years ago when a lorry overturned outside, blocking the door and trapping a number of lucky drinkers inside for the afternoon.

NEWALL
Spite

Newall Carr Side (one mile north of Otley)

- ✕ lunchtime (not Mon) and evening (not Sun and Mon)
-
- **Webster Yorkshire Bitter, Choice**

The story of how this hillside pub got its name is fascinating and a newspaper cutting on one of the walls tells it all. Simplified though, it stems back a century when a customer was rebuked for drinking at what was then called the Roebuck by the landlady of the adjacent Travellers Inn. His riposte was: "There's nobbut spite and malice up "ere." And Spite and Malice they became although the Malice is long gone and it was not until 1980 that Spite became the official name of this pub.

This is a comfortable haven with tasteful furnishings which display the personality of the landlady, Irene Law. Log fires warm the place in winter. Mrs Law has won many awards for her cooking and it is advisable to book for the small restaurant even at lunchtime. The pride of the menu is a ploughman's lunch with three cheeses, pate, quiche and home baked rolls. My own memories of eating there reflect some perfectly cooked vegetables to accompany a steak pie with a melting crust. Landlord, Eric Law, keeps a fine cellar as a complement and compliment to his wife's table. In summer the smart little garden is the perfect place to view Wharfedale and Otley Chevin.

OTLEY
Bay Horse

Market Place

- lunchtime
- rear yard
- **Tetley Mild, Bitter**

This is my favourite pub in a town where every one sells traditional ale. It is the empitome of the classic market town local, stashed away between main street and market place and the yards and snickets that abound in Otley. The mere look of the streetside frontage is enough to start the juices flowing – who needs aperitifs with a pub as attractive as this one.

The real delights start inside with the leaded lights of the doors and the tiles of the entrance hall. Turn right for the magic world of the tap room with its darts and dominoes and tiny servery; stay there if you wish, you will not be disappointed. Otherwise move into the lounge with its nooks, crannies and secret places fed by a lovely curving bar. Photographs on the walls reflect well the agrarian position of Otley by displaying scenes of farming in the area during the nineteenth century. A back door with more attractive glass opens to a suntrap of a pleasant back courtyard. A pub not to be missed.

RIPON
Water Rat

Bond End Green

- lunchtime and evening
- riverside balcony
- **Big End Yorkshire Rose Bitter, Old Lubrication; guest beers**

A new venture in an old pub with the former Alma being converted by Rodent Inns into another of the rat family. Also in the town is the One-Eyed Rat that was once the Lord Nelson! The Water Rat has been sensitively extended as befits a riverside pub in a town of great antiquity in which the Cathedral of St Wilfred dominates. The pub is near enough to the Wakeman's House in the market square to hear the sound of the horn fanfare blown every night at nine o' clock – "Except the Lord keep the city the Wakeman waketh in vain" as the motto says.

The setting is the thing with this pub, overlooking the River Skell with its riverside walk which passes below and is linked by a gate to an attractive balcony. Summer afternoons on the river do not have to mean boating, they can be better appreciated with a pint of Bill Witty's Big End ale, he being one of the partners of the rodentia. The bar serves two areas, linked but clearly defined and there is also a snug, the whole place well decorated, interesting and comfortable. Good food is important here and there is a varied selection of meals where local produce plays a big part.

SKIPTON
Royal Shepherd

Canal Street

✕ lunchtime

Hartley XB; Marston Pedigree; Whitbread Castle Eden Ale, Trophy Bitter, Strong Country Bitter

≹ Skipton

This uniquely named pub is alongside the Springs Canal, an arm of the Leeds and Liverpool. The name is derived from the now defunct Order of the Golden Fleece. It is a terrace-end set of cottages which have been sensitively renovated rather than in the usual Whitbread style. Skipton, as befits one of Yorkshire's best market towns, ought to have a splendid choice of pubs but sadly this is not so; the Royal Shepherd stands out well above an indifferent crowd.

It has three rooms all with a purpose and individual character. The pleasant lounge bar contains a mirror from the former Bentley brewery of Woodlesford, some long cast-iron tables, a set of photographs of the town at the turn of the century and a resident cat searching out the warmest corner. The parlour is a shrine to cricket and in particular the Church Institute CC which has its headquarters at the pub; the snug, rather plain, is the family room. The landlord will tell you that this is Gloria Hunniford's favourite pub – there's a recommendation.

SLAIDBURN
Hark to Bounty

Tel: (020 06) 246
On B6478 eight miles west of Hellifield

- ✕ lunchtime and evening
- forecourt
-
- **Moorhouse's Pendle Witches Brew; John Smith Bitter**

Slaidburn is the gateway to the Trough of Bowland, provided you are travelling from Yorkshire. It is set in some of the most delightful country in the Pennine foothills and the pity of it is that Lancashire has claimed it since 1974. However, this in no way diminishes the Hark to Bounty. It was originally known as the Dog Inn and in 1875 became one of several "Hark to..." inns to be found in the borders. They all have the same foundation if not the same name. Squire Wrigglesworth was the master of the local hunt and Bounty was his favourite hound. When they picked up the scent of the fox, Bounty was the loudest and the Squire would call out "Hark [listen] to Bounty".

The Swainmote court was held here to deal with offenders of the laws of the Royal Forest of Bowland, and the court room and jury box are retained on the first floor. The welcoming lounge has a Victorian feel with prints and plates of the period on its walls. Furniture is stylish and comfortable and there is an open fire. Food is popular, with some good cheese and sausages and well filled sandwiches. Bed and breakfast is available and fishing can be arranged on a nearby resevoir.

STARBOTTON
Fox & Hounds

Tel: (075 676) 269
On B6160, 20 miles north of Skipton

- ✕ lunchtime and evening
-
-
- **Taylor Landlord; Theakston Best Bitter, Old Peculier, Younger Scotch**

A splendid Dales inn dating from 1834 with an amusing sign that shows a hunt in progress with the fox riding one of the leading horses. Occasionally, even the hunting fraternity displays a sense of humour. The limestone village of Starbotton is perfectly placed for walking the Dales, particularly to some other splendid pubs – the Falcon at Arncliffe (qv) is a good stiff climb over the hill to more than 1500 feet, but the George at Hubberholme (qv) is a comfortable evening saunter along the riverside.

The interior of the pub is old fashioned and comfortable with flagged floors and an enormous open fireplace which roars away in winter. A new kitchen has been installed and the food is excellent with an emphasis on local produce including game. Accommodation is available, although what I remember as massive bedrooms more suited to dancing in than sleeping, have now been foreshortened by the addition of bathrooms. What you will remember about Starbotton are the views.

TADCASTER
Angel & White Horse

Bridge Street

✕ lunchtime

Samuel Smith Old Brewery Bitter, Museum Ale

As the name implies there were once two pubs – coaching inns – on this site and a rather complicated history brings us up to date with the present one which opened a few years ago and acts as a flagship for the Samuel Smith brewery just behind. Tadcaster can count its brewing history back at least five centuries and "Sam's" dating from 1758 is not only the oldest brewery in the town but in the county as well.

The pub's facade is impressive and genuinely Georgian and whilst the inside is completely new it has been done in a dignified and traditional manner. The long room with its alcoves and partitions loops around a half circular bar and the whole is pleasantly decked out in fine wood panelling. From the back is a picture window that looks out on the stables and the brewery yard. Lunchtime food is good plain cooking and substantial.

THRESHFIELD
Old Hall

Tel: (0756) 752441
B6160/B6265 one mile west of Grassington

✕ lunchtime and evening

Taylor Best Bitter, Landlord; Younger Scotch; guest beer

The back part of the inn gives it its name – it is the oldest inhabited building in Wharfedale. The setting is rather pretty with some good trees around and an aviary in the side garden where tables are set out. Inside three rooms are linked and a recent refurbishment has done nothing to spoil the old fashioned style of the place. Pots hang from the roof and the white walls are simply and interestingly decorated. Children are welcome in the conservatory.

Food is important here but not to the detriment of the other facilities. Local produce plays its part with game prominent in season – wood pigeon pie, game casserole – and some simple yet excellent traditional dishes such as Yorkshire puddings with onion gravy and large haddock fillets in batter. They say that steak and kidney pie is the best seller. There are bedrooms available and the location is ideal for walking holidays.

WHITEWELL
Inn at Whitewell

Tel: (020 08) 222
Forest of Bowland, about five miles north west of Clitheroe

✕ lunchtime and evening

Moorhouse's Premier Bitter, Pendle Witches Brew

This is a fascinating place and the owner is no less than HM the Queen in her capacity as Duke of Lancaster. This is another pub lost to Lancashire by the local government reorganisation of 1974. It was originally the manor house where the keeper of the King's deer park lived in the fourteenth century and was owned by the Townsley family from the nineteenth century. There have been alterations and extensions to the inn in both the Georgian and Victorian periods but it retains some fine carved stone fireplaces and original oak beams.

The whole building has a feel of a country house rather than an inn and the high standard of furnishings and decor testify to this. The lounge has some splendid gate-legged tables and tapestry-backed settles, old prints adorn the walls and the centrepiece is a imposing stone fireplace. The public bar does well for pub games enthusiasts with shove-ha'penny, darts, dominoes and a slot machine from the thirties. There is even a piano. Food ranges from the simple: home-made pies, sandwiches, some good cheeses; to the exotic: duck breast with kumquats and carpet bags of pastry stuffed with an assortment of seafood.

There is plenty of drinking space outdoors and the inn has five miles of fishing rights on the Hodder. In the same premises are a wine merchant, a clothes shop and an art gallery and there is overnight accommodation.

WIGHILL
White Swan

Main Street, two miles north of Tadcaster

- lunchtime and evening
- benches at front; rear courtyard
- **John Smith Bitter; Theakston Best Bitter, XB, Old Peculier**

There are two bars serving several rooms and a tiny nook alongside one of them. This is an unspoilt pub of real character that has just changed hands for a substantial sum after many years in the same family and there is plenty of evidence that the high standards set before will be maintained. The exterior is a delight with its whitewashed front and stables and outbuildings at the back.

All the small rooms have their own personalities and the locals tend to foregather in the front bar on the left, regarding it as their own club. No worry though, there is plenty of other space to spread into. The whole place is a happy mix of old attractive furniture, interesting pictures and *objets d'art*. Lunchtime snacks and meals are substantial and whilst the restaurant is new it appears to be doing well.

*** * * LATE ENTRY * * ***

BECKINGDALE
Woolpack

Main Street, three miles west of Hotton

- lunchtime
- tables on forecourt
- **Ephraim's Mild, Bitter**
- Skipdale

This is one of the four best known pubs in Britain yet it remains a quiet unspoilt country local frequented only by the 20 or so folk who live in the dale. They drink enough however to make a living for the crotchety landlord Amos Brearley, his live-in partner the placid Henry Wilks, and a barmaid, the delightful Dolly Skilbeck who disguises her posh voice by dropping an aitch every now and then. This is a one room pub, quite small with no special features other than a large open fire place and some wood panelled walls. There are some characters amongst the locals and more conspiracies have been plotted here than were ever contemplated in the upstairs room of the Olde White Hart in Hull (qv).

Try also the Malt Shovel.

ABERFORD
Arabian Horse

Great North Road (old A1)

✕ lunchtime (not Sun)

garden with children's playground

Home Mild; McEwan 80/-; Younger Scotch, No 3

This pub has a unique name and dates from 1850 when the first Arabian racehorses arrived in Britain. They were being taken to training stables in Wensleydale but the beck flooded and the horses were stranded. So the owner of the Bay Horse, as was, having seen the splendid thoroughbreds, changed it to the Arabian Horse. The pub dates from 1770 and one of its pair of magnificent stone fireplaces is almost as old. It was only rediscovered in 1975 when an inquisitive landlord chipped away some of the dreary Victorian wood surround that had covered it for a century or more. The fireplaces stand guard at both ends of a comfortable lounge set out in the "shop" style and provide essential warmth in winter and a talking point throughout the year. The large tap room to the rear is popular with darts, dominoes, shove ha'penny and pool players.

The Arabian Horse stands on the old Great North Road facing the green of one of the most attractive villages in the Leeds district. There is much to see here including Victorian almshouses; arches and a bell from coaching days; some iron age entrenchments and a triumphal arch built to commemorate "Liberty in N. America." Lotherton Hall, a Victorian mansion with a bird garden is but two miles away.

ALMONDBURY
Castle Hill Hotel

Tel: (0484) 421473
Lumb Lane

✕ lunchtime and evening

Tetley Mild, Bitter; Theakston Best Bitter, XB, Old Peculier

Castle Hill is Huddersfield's most recognisable landmark and the pub of the same name stands close to the 1897 Victoria Tower. On the hill itself stand the remains of an iron age fort dating back to 300 BC which was sacked by the Romans and brought back into use ten centuries on by King Stephen. In early Victorian days there were gooseberry gardens and a house that sold ginger beer to the many visitors. The first hotel dates from 1853.

A recent refurbishment of the pub has created two rooms out of one – a lounge and a public bar – and there is also a restaurant. Coal fires heat the place and there is a general air of uncomplicated comfort. Meals in the bar are simple and Sunday lunches are popular. The panoramic views and location can hardly be bettered and there are safe acres for kids and dogs to roam in.

BARDSEY
Bingley Arms

Tel: (0937) 72462
Church Lane (just off the A58)

× lunchtime and evening

Tetley Mild, Bitter

According to church records there has been a pub on this site since the tenth century although the Guinness Book of Records is slightly enigmatic about its claims to be England's oldest inn. Up to the middle of the eighteenth century it was called the Priest's Inn and takes it present name from the family who owned the land. Nikolaus Pevsner has much to say in his volume on the buildings of the West Riding about the Saxon church of All Hallows but nothing about the Bingley Arms. What is certain is that there are ancient parts of this building, it does have an interesting history and it is still a good pub to visit.

There is a traditional, well laid out tap room entered from the left and a large comfortable and rather quaint lounge. Upstairs is a well patronised restaurant that looks to the immediate area for its produce and is all the better for it. The roofing timbers have been exposed recently and it really is a rather splendid hall. Around the back a terraced beer garden captures the early evening sunshine. The pub is well situated for a visit before and after the Wetherby races.

BINGLEY
Brown Cow

Tel :(0274) 569582
Ireland Bridge

- ✕ lunchtime and Tue – Sat evenings
- ▦
- **Taylor Golden Best, Best Bitter, Landlord, Ram Tam**
- ⇌ Bingley

The Brown Cow has its origins in the seventeenth century but it was rebuilt between the wars and is an excellent example of the smaller "improved" public house. Its history is interesting for it was a regular venue for official meetings and occasionally unlawful ones when the local chartists made it their headquarters. In 1753 the Keighley and Bradford Turnpike Trust met here. It was also the petty sessions court and in an upstairs room a private school was established and survived the 1870 Education Act which provided for universal schooling. It had its own brewery until the Great War.

This rather smart pub with its picture postcard frontage is happily set alongside the River Aire at Ireland Bridge, the town's only road crossing. A pleasant bar serves a large open area which has many secret corners; it is an interesting room with comfortable armchairs and some panelling taken from a redundant church. The small dining room is decorated in the style of the period. Outside is a most attractive terraced drinking area overlooked by high trees and taking full advantage of the steep sides of the valley. The food is substantial with some excellent if rather expensive sandwiches and Taylor's beers are always kept in peak condition. Jazz nights on Mondays are always well patronised.

BRADFORD
Cock & Bottle

93 Barkerend Road

- ✕ lunchtime
- **Tetley Mild, Bitter**
- ⇌ Bradford (Foster Square)

This Tetley Heritage Inn is a late Victorian gem although its history goes back much further than the present building. There are tales of its involvement in the Civil War during the siege of Bradford, but records of an alehouse here only date from the early eighteenth century. The name Cock and Bottle was taken about 1822 and is thought to mean that it sold both draught and bottled beers, the word "cock" meaning a spigot or tap. The frontage and interior were rebuilt in 1862 and it has remained largely unchanged since then. The pub has theatrical connections and many prints and programmes of great age are displayed on the walls. It was a favourite of Florrie Ford when she appeared in the town.

A myriad of small rooms remain, with some splendid etched glass, mirrors and woodwork. The fine main bar contains lockable boxes which were used by merchants to keep their samples in – or their top hats when they were drinking – and one compartment housed an antique central heating system. Between this room and the large music room, where live entertainment regularly takes place, are two tiny snugs, unspoilt examples of pub Victoriana. To the back is a large, airy and thriving tap room. All tales to the effect that there is a tunnel between here and Bradford Cathedral just down the road are, in my view, false. But it does make a good talking point.

Oakleigh

4 Oak Avenue, Manningham

- ✕ lunchtime
- ▣
- **Marston Pedigree; Old Mill Traditional Bitter; Taylor Best Bitter, Landlord; Theakston XB; Thwaites Best Bitter; guest beer**
- ⇌ Frizinghall

What was obviously one of the mansions of the Victorian wool barons in leafy Manningham eventually became a hotel. In more recent days it turned public house and in the hands of Bob Tucker, now at the Laurel in Robin Hoods Bay (qv) it was one of the first genuine free houses in Bradford and a pioneer of the real ale revival. Its attractive setting is in a good location, convenient for Lister Park and Cartwright Hall Art Gallery.

The main bar is large with identifiable areas and it opens up to an excellent garden where children are welcome. The clientele is mixed and it is a popular calling off point for real ale drinkers from all parts of West Yorkshire. Young people find it attractive despite the lack of a juke box. Food is well prepared and often more than adequate.

Ring o' Bells

18 Bolton Road

- ✕ lunchtime
- **Tetley Mild, Bitter**
- ⇌ Bradford (Foster Square)

There is a general air of comfort about this well sited pub just that far out of the city centre to be able to park yet near enough to be able to use as a refuge from the rigours of shopping or after the cinema. Its white rendered stone block front stands out across Foster Square and closer examination shows up some excellent windows including a couple from former owners Melbourne of Leeds. A door to the left displays "Saloon Bar" but this is long closed and is used as a store.

The bar area is rather crowded making it difficult to appreciate the splendid solid wood bar curving gracefully to face both parts of the large lounge. This room is full of good dark wood screens with fine etched glass, some original, some replacement, but all fitting well into the scheme of things which includes comfortable furniture and an interesting collection of Victorian pictures. A superb snug is tucked away behind the bar with its own hatch servery; this is a handsome room and, with good reason, is nearly always busy. Lunchtime meals are of the "chips with everything" style but they are generous and nothing costs more than £2.

Shoulder of Mutton

Kirkgate

✕ lunchtime

⊛

⊟ **Samuel Smith Old Brewery Bitter**

⇌ Bradford (Exchange and Foster Square)

The suggestion that there is a beer garden attached to the Shoulder of Mutton is usually met with incredulity. But it's there tucked away behind this city centre terraced pub to provide a haven for busy office workers and shoppers, visitors even, during the hot sunny days of summer. It is probably the best urban pub garden in Britain, with a magnificent display of plants, shrubs and flowers and has won awards including several in the Pub Gardens of Britain competition. It is advisable to beat the midday rush and secure a seat in this suntrap.

It has other qualities aside from the garden and in not too clement days the several rooms are cosy and welcoming, the snug by the side of the bar in particular. Good value lunches are available here with regular favourites of pies, flans and salads and specials like Old Brewery casserole and, rare for Bradford, curry made with pork. They do not own a microwave and nothing costs more than £2. The Shoulder is a handsome pub, in its time it was a coaching inn, the present building dating from 1825.

DENSHAW
Rams Head (Owd Tupps)

Ripponden Road (A672)

- **Taylor Landlord; Theakston Best Bitter, XB, Old Peculier; guest beers**

It is possible to get cut off here during heavy snows and I suppose in a pub slung high on the roof of the Pennines that this is to be expected. I can remember, in my days as a BBC news producer, reporting the various roads closed across to Lancashire and wondering whether anyone had got locked in such a pub. The Rams Head would not be too bad a place to face that predicament. Yet its isolation is part of its charm for on sunny summer evenings I can think of no better view than up the Tame valley into the very heart of the hills. This is border country.

The low stone building with its thick walls is well protected against the elements and inside three small rooms open out from the bar area each with its own personality. My particular favourite is the tap room to the left – wooden seating, stylish old tables, a roaring coal fire, good crack and a pint straight from the barrel. Oh to be locked in! Here the gravity system of dispense is retained and the casks are stillaged behind the bar with steel jugs used to fill the glasses. It may be stating the obvious but this is in the heart of good walking country with the Pennine Way nearby, but the distance to the next pub is something that needs another pint to contemplate.

DEWSBURY
Market House

Church Street

- lunchtime
- **Tetley Mild, Bitter**
- Dewsbury

There has been a pub on this site for centuries but the present one dates from 1902 and is an excellent example of Yorkshire craftmanship, built in local stone to an ornate style with interesting gables, dormers and high chimneys and, in complete contrast, some art nouveau windows. Tetleys made this one of their Heritage Inns and it is easy to understand why.

The layout is original with a tap room to the front, tall, light and airy, warmed by a splendid cast iron fireplace and served by an impressive bank of five handpumps. Hatches from the bar service the corridor drinking area, a fair expectation for a West Riding, turn of the century pub; and also the back lounge or snug which is comfortable and full of interesting photographs of old Dewsbury. The pub's history can be found on the walls along with documents relating to it. A spotless gem.

ELDWICK
Dick Hudsons

Otley Road, High Eldwick

✕ lunchtime and evening

Tetley Mild, Bitter

This is one of Yorkshire's best known pubs, originally called the Fleece but known to millions as Dick Hudsons which is now its official name. Richard Hudson was the licensee from 1850 to 1878, taking over from his father Tommy. It was a favourite day out spot for the mill workers of the West Riding towns and was famous for its ham and eggs cooked in an 18 inch frying pan and served all day. It has literary connections with both J B Priestley and Howard Spring writing of it and enjoying its facilities. Spring found a place for it in his novel Fame is the Spur.

The reputation for good food continues and in particular the Sunday lunches are good value. This is a Tetley "Wayfarers Inn" one of a group of pubs that cater specially for families and there is a well equipped children's room, a family conservatory with magnificent views over the Aire valley, and a children's menu. The rest of the pub is traditional and comfortable and often busy with both car trade and walkers – it is on the edge of Rombalds Moor, the "father" of Ilkley Moor.

ELLAND
Barge & Barrel

Park Road

✕ lunchtime and evening until 8 pm

Marston Burton Best Bitter, Pedigree; Oak Best Bitter, Old Oak Ale, West Riding Tyke; Taylor Landlord; guest beers

A foursquare building backing on to the Elland basin of the Calder and Hebble navigation. It was built to service the now long gone Elland railway station. After the line closed it led a chequered life for some years but since 1985 it has been in the personal control of two directors of the West Riding Brewery Company – its only tied house. They have restored it to its former Victorian grandeur as far as it is possible to do so. And they have gone one further by extending it to cater for adults who are accompanied by children.

The main lounge loops round a horseshoe bar and there is a snug and a games room on either side of the entrance. To the left is the family area with a selection of games including a very popular ball pool – a sort of swimming pool you don't get wet in. The food is excellent and there is a kid's menu as well as bar snacks and hot meals every day. The speciality is a Tom Pudding, a Yorkshire pudding filled with melting lumps of braised beef – named after the compartment boats that carried coal along the navigations of the West Riding. The beers include their own West Riding Tyke, specially brewed by Oak Brewery in Birkenhead after a fire destroyed their own brewery in Meltham.

GLASSHOUGH-TON
Rock Inn

Rock Hill

Ward Darley Dark Mild, Darley Thorne Best Bitter, Kirby Ale (occasional)

Castleford

This, be warned, is the headquarters of the Yorkshire Subterranean Society which may speak volumes for the standard of the cellar work that goes into serving such excellent quality ale. It is a strange contradiction that such a society should flourish in what is basically a mining village. It also probably explains why I have yet to find this pub anything but busy.

If you enter this foursquare, turn of the century, brick-built pub by the door from the car park you will see it has glass panels marked "Jug". More evidence of a small jug and bottle department is still there inside although the counter and office have gone. A pity. Many of the original features of this village local are still with us, however.

A busy, noisy tap room at the front is served by a three-sided bar that also copes with the large lounge and corridor. Opposite the tap room is a haven of a snug which, like the lounge, has lots of interest on its walls. There are Victorian posters for Gilbert and Sullivan operettas, sets of cigarette cards, celebratory newspapers and maps of caves the Subterraneans have explored. An original Yorkshire range warms one end of the lounge and a large iron fireplace burns logs at the other. Pool is played in an upstairs room and there is folk music on Wednesdays.

BEER AND CRICKET

Bobby Peel, the Yorkshire and England cricketer became the landlord of the Commercial Inn on Churwell Hill in Morley after he ceased to play the first class game in 1897. During his career he took 1550 wickets for his county and 102 in 20 Test matches, all against Australia. In nine seasons he took 100 wickets, once taking eight for 12 against Nottinghamshire; he scored six centuries and in 1896 did the double. But his liking for beer led to the end of his cricket career and his subsequent entry into the licensed trade. He was sacked by the formidable Yorkshire captain, Lord Hawke, the season after the two of them had broken the Yorkshire eighth wicket partnership record with a score of 292 against Warwickshire to which Peel contributed 210 not out. It was said that he celebrated by urinating on the pitch but this tale appears to have been discounted. In the following season however Bobby marked a century against Leicestershire with a booze up of heroic proportions and the following day he was still considerably hung over. He commenced bowling by running towards the sight screen and his fellow players had to turn him round. This was too much for his Lordship who forbade him to play for Yorkshire again. Bobby Peel died in 1941 at the age of 84. The Commercial is known as the "top 'ole" because it is the top pub of three on Churwell Hill.

HALIFAX
Shears Inn

Paris Gates, Boys Lane

- ✕ lunchtime
- (garden)
- **Taylor Best Bitter, Landlord; Younger Scotch, No 3; guest beers**
- ⇌ Halifax

First things first – find the place! It is tucked away in the valley bottom just five minutes walk from the town centre behind the Halifax Town football ground, the Shay, and just over the railway. It is only difficult to find the first six times. It is really a village inn and although it is shut in by dark satanic mills, it was here before them and is possibly 250 years old. The bar is a welcome place and good value food is available. The landlord, Jim Tierney, selects his guest beers with care and likes to move throughout the country for them.

Despite its apparent isolation the Shears is never short of activity. It has been used as a location for a couple of feature films and any number of sports clubs have their headquarters here – cricket, football and hockey clubs and the Halifax Harriers – and a choir as well.

Woodcock

213 Gibbet Street

- ✕ lunchtime and evening
- **Marston Pedigree ;Taylor Landlord ; Theakston Best Bitter, XB, Old Peculier ; guest beers**

An ale house with no pretensions: it sets out its manifesto to supply good beer with occasional forays across the nation for its guests, and plain but substantial food and deserves your vote. Don't expect frills, don't look for antique furniture; the best you are likely to find by way of decor is a collection of beer mats, bottles and pump clips from the many dozens of breweries that have sold their wares here. Some leaded lights remain from the days when this was a Ramsden's of Halifax pub called the Bowling Green. The food here is straightforward with some noteworthy sandwiches and hearty hot meals. Occasionally live music sessions are held and the records on the juke box include some fine "oldies".

HARTSHEAD
Gray Ox

Tel: (0274) 872845
15 Hartshead Lane

- ✖ lunchtime (not Mon) and evenings
- garden with children's playground
- **Ruddles Best Bitter, County; Webster Green Label Best, Yorkshire Bitter**

They look after kids well here in this rural pub which is almost within an arrow shot's distance of where Robin Hood is supposed to have been buried. The odd but not incorrect spelling of the name is said to be due to a signwriter making a mistake some 80 years ago which has stuck. The garden offers some superb views and barbecues are held here during the summer. For the children there is an inflated castle and in the family room some good toys including a rocking horse and a blackboard. Food for the youngsters is more imaginative than in most places and they can choose from their own menu.

The building dates back to the seventeenth century and the public rooms are relaxed and comfortable with a fireplace in one that has been listed as of historic significance. The restaurant is always busy and it is advisable to book; the portions are enormous and the menu includes a 32–ounce steak

HAWORTH
Fleece Inn

Main Street

- ✖ lunchtime
- **Taylor Golden Best, Best Bitter, Landlord, Ram Tam (winter only)**

It is a good ten minute uphill stride from the town station on the Keighley and Worth Valley railway, where you may also have sampled a local brew in the buffet car. Home is downhill. The Fleece never made any claims that Branwell Brontë drank here although he might well have done. It used to show its fame as the watering hole for the cast of the "Railway Children" film, but now the comfortable family room on the right of the entrance houses a spoof Brontë exhibition. It upset some of the more staid disciples at first, but it's harmless and helps to restore a bit of balance in a town that occasionally fills out with pretentious folk who wouldn't know a wuthering height if they fell off one.

The main bar in this one time coaching inn is stone-flagged and has recently been opened out a little but to no detriment. Locals prevail but visitors are welcome. To the left is a small games area and upstairs is a function room where many local societies meet. The spin-off from this is obvious and the Fleece stands out as a centre of village life.

HEATH
Kings Arms

Tel: (0924) 377527
Heath Common, one mile east of Wakefield off A655

✕ lunchtime and evening

▪

▪ **Clark GSB, Traditional Bitter, Burglar Bill, Wakefield Ale, Hammerhead; Taylor Landlord; Tetley Bitter**

Heath is worth the visit if only to savour the atmosphere of a perfectly preserved West Yorkshire village which comes as something of a surprise being so near to Wakefield. Architects like James Paine and John Carr have work here and the two large houses fit in well with the smaller gatehouses and cottages and, of course, the village inn.

It is eighteenth century and retains much of its original ambience including gas lighting and stone flagged floors in some of the rooms. The main bar has a splendid fireplace burning great logs and spreading its warmth into the winter evening. There is wood panelling throughout and the furniture is assorted and antique to give a delightful expression of casualness. On the right of the doorway is a tiny, stand-up snug in which three would be a crowd and to the rear are small quiet rooms where the world might be a million miles away. Tranquil is a good word to describe the Kings Arms. Bar food is substantial and the restaurant next door specialises in Yorkshire dishes.

HOLMFIRTH
Rose & Crown (Nook)

Victoria Square

▪ courtyard

▪ **Samuel Smith Old Brewery Bitter; Stones Best Bitter; Taylor Landlord, Ram Tam; Tetley Mild, Bitter; Younger No 3; guest beers**

The tales told about this place are legion. Holmfirth may be the heart of the "Last of the Summer Wine" country but the "Nook" will certainly be the last of the real pubs. If ever a pub should be labelled enigmatic this is it. Finding the place for a start is a job in itself and asking for the Rose and Crown will do you no good for everyone in the town knows it as the "Nook". Even the football team is called Nook City AFC. It is tucked away in a tiny square off Hollowgate and no more than a few yards from the main flow of folk looking for Compo and Nora. Better things await in the "Nook'.

It is, not to paint too fine a picture, a basic pub. Its spaces and rooms run away from one another in a splendid confusion that gives it real atmosphere. At one time the pub piano was in the gents! There are some interesting touches including what I am told are panelled ceilings common to the Holme Valley area, but you won't be visiting this place to discuss the merits of architectural design. The beer is all important along with the crack and the man behind both is David Roberts, an Irishman of note and recently retired as a schoolteacher. Folk musicians are at home here particularly during the Holmfirth Folk Festival every July. As the "Good Beer Guide" says: "...a local legend in its own lifetime."

HONLEY
Coach & Horses

Eastgate

- ✕ lunchtime (Mon to Fri) and Mon evenings
- forecourt
- **Bass Mild XXXX, Light 5 Star; Draught Bass; Stones Best Bitter**
- ⇌ Honley

This is a splendidly positioned pub in the centre of Honley that attracts locals and visitors alike. It dates from the early eighteenth century, was a coaching inn and takes its place in the history of the Luddites. It is known locally as "Henry's" after a former landlord. The present incumbent, David Woodhead, is a great traditionalist and the pub speaks volumes for his efforts including the retention of dark mild ale despite the efforts of the brewery to remove it. The main bar serves lots of different areas and the appeal is to all ages and groups – the comforts are manifold with delightful furnishings, interesting wall decor and excellent food. The situation appeals too, on the edge of the Pennines in the middle of "pratty flowers" land with Holmfirth "nobbut a cockstride" away.

HUDDERSFIELD
Shoulder of Mutton

Neale Road, Lockwood
Closed Mon-Fri lunchtime

Taylor Landlord, Tetley Mild, Bitter; Theakston XB; Thwaites Bitter; guest beers

Lockwood

This old fashioned pub is at the top (which in Yorkshire means "end') of a cobbled street just off the Meltham road. It only opens in the evening through the week and is often extremely busy although the atmosphere seems relaxed and homely. The three small rooms open out from a main drinking area in front of the bar. They are panelled in walnut and the lighting is rather subdued. Children are welcome and there is a popular garden. In the tap room to the left bar skittles is one of the pub games. The juke box has its devotees and rightly so for here are the Stones, Bob Dylan, the Beatles, Buddy Holly and none of your present day rubbish, says he showing his age.

Slubbers Arms

Halifax Old Road

lunchtime

Marston Pedigree; Old Mill Traditional Bitter; Taylor Best Bitter; guest beers

This unique name for a pub comes from a job in the textile trade – a slubber twisted yarn after combing to prepare it for spinning. This mid-Victorian pub was originally owned by Peter Marsland and Son, the Huddersfield brewers who, having been taken over by Wilsons of Manchester in 1889, continued brewing in their own name until 1926. The Wilson checker board sign is still on the outside of this street-corner, wedge-shaped pub although it has been a free house for some time.

The shape of the servery reflects the external appearance and the two sides of the main bar have their own devotees. Characters abound in the Slubbers, not least the landlord, David Green, whose anecdotes are worth a pint or two. There are coal fires to add to the atmosphere and a tiny tap room houses the pub games.

JACKSON BRIDGE
Red Lion

Tel: (0484) 683499
Sheffield Road (A616)

✕ lunchtime and early evening

❀

⊷

⊕ **Marston Pedigree; Tetley Mild, Bitter**

You will not be able to avoid being told that you are in the "Last of the Summer Wine" country, the business having almost reached the same heights as "The Sound of Music" did in the Salzkammergut. Don't let this deter you from visiting this cosy old inn in an attractive Pennine village – you will also find here the White Horse Inn where the television programme has a higher profile. The Red Lion is run by a mother and son combination, the Oscrofts, with a good deal of style.

The comforts are self evident and run to an accent on china – on display in the pub; meals served on it; and even china cup and saucers in the rooms. The menu includes many unusual dishes; the prawn and pineapple starter is highly recommended. The are are nine letting bedrooms all with television and some with bathrooms. Views from the garden over the village and into the Pennines are superb. Music is of the owner's choice and ranges from Madonna to Mozart. There is a resident ghost, Chippy Brook, a former landlord who like many other folk is reluctant to leave the pub.

KIRKHEATON
Beaumont Arms

Church Lane

✕ lunchtime

❀

⊕ **Tetley Mild, Bitter**

Kirkheaton received a mention in the Domesday Book: "...the village in the garden, the church in the hollow..." and it could have added "with a country pub tucked away for company." The church is dominant but the pairing make good calendar copy and are linked by a tunnel. The cellar of the pub contains more than beer; it has a cell with a bed, table and shelves, presuming that at some time it was also the village lock-up. They call the Beaumont Arms – the name comes from the family that owned most of the land hereabouts – the "Kirkstile" or "Kirksteel". The Beaumonts have been around for some centuries and there is a chapel and several monuments dedicated to them in the church.

A small room by the pub's front door houses a selection of brass bells that gives you a hint of what is to come. The magnificent polished oak bar serves this room and the adjacent lounge and open drinking area. Here there is a remarkable collection of more than 200 horse, pony and even elephant brasses; more can be found elsewhere – all kept sparklingly clean. Other items add to the interest, such as jugs, candlesticks and plates. The games room, with its attractive wood settles, is not missed out with sporting prints and old photographs of the area. Upstairs is the Long Chamber, once a court room which seems to confirm the lock-up theory, and now used for functions. It has a marvellous fireplace and yet more brass.

LEDSHAM
Chequers

Tel: (0977) 683135
Holly Rood Lane (one mile west of A1)
Closed on Sundays

- ✕ lunchtime and evening
-
-
- **Theakston Best Bitter; Younger Scotch, IPA, No 3**

This is the only pub in the West Riding (or even West Yorkshire) that has a six-day licence. It is a throwback to Victorian days when on a Sunday afternoon after a fierce session some fellows transgressed the limits of decency by using the garden as a toilet and offended the lady of the manor. This is an estate pub and feudal law rules although I suspect that no-one has tested the licensing waters recently. Curiosities apart, and at one time it was an undertakers, this is a splendid village inn in a delightful setting.

Its ivy covered outward appearance gives a taste of delights to come, and the gaggle of tiny rooms splashed around the compact little central bar provides something for everyone. There is a nice local feel about it, particularly in the early evening, and it is just far enough away from Leeds to be spared the great bores of today talking about themselves. Children are made to feel at home here, the beer is always in condition and the upstairs restaurant has a fine reputation. I was here on Spring Bank Holiday Monday in 1989 at about 4 pm. It was about 80 degrees in the shade; the IPA went down a treat and I thought: "This time last year this place would have been shut." A curse on social reformers.

LEEDS
Adelphi

Leeds Bridge, Hunslet Road

✕ weekday lunchtime

Tetley Mild, Bitter

Leeds

It will be difficult to find a more elaborate "tap" than the Adelphi, standing as it does in the shadow of Tetley's brewery. The setting does a lot for it with the gracefully curving granite facade making the most of its corner site. According to the sign above the entrance the landlord is "licensed to brew" and whilst it is

A corner of the Adelphi, Leeds

many years since this was the case it remains one of many conversation pieces the Adelphi has to offer.

Inside is a myriad of delights with a selection of four rooms and a spacious drinking corridor which is set off by a splendid staircase. The whole affair is a mass of polished mahogany, etched glass and sparkling tiles. At lunchtime the place is always busy with workers from the brewery and other firms in the developing area of the waterfront and in the evening it takes off as a meeting place for societies, trade unions, sports clubs and the like. Regular music sessions featuring the famed Ed O'Donnell jazz band are held in the upstairs room on Saturday nights.

Trad jazz at the Adelphi, Saturday night

Albion

86 Armley Road

✕ weekday lunchtime

Tetley Bitter

This pub is, I am certain, the only one in Yorkshire to appear in all 17 editions of the "Good Beer Guide". It was also one of the first winners of a CAMRA Pub Preservation Group award after a tasteful renovation which gave it Tetley Heritage Inn status. This end of Armley Road has been by-passed and whilst the lunchtime trade is constant from the many factories around, the evening brings a crowd of loyal regulars from good distances. They know good beer and a good pub.

Walkers of Warrington were the former owners of what was once two pubs and their splendid tiled sign is now displayed again after burial under some of the ubiquitous Allied plank decor. The frontage with its glorious tiling and local brick received recognition when it was chosen as the archetypal urban pub for models on Hornby railways. Inside the main bar is in the West Riding shop style – high and airy with a coal fire and some good traditional furniture and the long bar counter running parallel to the front. Two hatches from the back of the bar serve a snug to the right and a comfortable lounge to the left. A pool room is tucked away at the back and there is a meeting room upstairs.

Eagle Tavern

Tel: (0532) 457146
North Street

✕ lunchtime

walled yard

Taylor Dark Mild, Golden Best, Best Bitter, Landlord, Ram Tam; guest beers and cider

This is one of the oldest, comparatively unspoilt pubs in Leeds. Others claim greater longevity but brother, look at them now! Its Georgian origins are patent and it actually dates from 1826 when it was a private house for the Bussey family who were master builders. Six years later, taking advantage of the Wellington Beerhouse Act, a licence was obtained and the Eagle opened its doors to the public. Its popularity has ebbed and flowed over the years and it has flown some interesting flags of ownership – McQuats of Meadow Lane, Samuel Smith, CAMRA Investments and now Timothy Taylor of Keighley.

The choice of rooms is the large functional tap room to the left with its long bar, wooden settles and sporting photographs, or right to the plush lounge, recently extended to include two cosy alcoves where part of the bar used to be. Photographs of the area around the turn of the century and a history of the pub decorate the walls. There is live music at the weekends with the ubiquitous Ed O'Donnell jazz band on Sunday lunchtime. There are several letting bedrooms at most reasonable rates but beware room seven – it is supposed to be haunted!

Garden Gate

Waterloo Road, Hunslet

✕ weekday lunchtime

Tetley Mild, Bitter

I think I coined the term "a palace of refreshment" although my conscience tells me it may have come from someone else. Either way, the description belongs to the Garden Gate if to no other pub. The pleasures start as you arrive at the magnificent terracotta-faced frontage with its etched windows. Through the door, and after noting the splendid mosaic floor, either discover the innermost secrets of the tap room to the left with its ornate bar and the feeling that nothing has changed for a century, or go on to the corridor where the serious drinking is done. Here the macho drinker eschews the noxious practice of necking a bottle and sups pints of Tets from a sleever. They also ignore the multi-choice of rooms – four in all – to stand and see, and be seen. The corridor pub is of Yorkshire and the Garden Gate, all glass, dark wood, tiles of cream and eau de nil, brass and conversation, is Yorkshire. They travel here from London, 200 miles up the motorway, just for lunchtime sessions on a Sunday and say it's worth it. For me the five miles from my home is five miles too far.

Whitelocks

Tel: (0532) 453950
Turks Head Yard, Briggate

- lunchtime and evening until 7.30 pm
- alleyway with seats and tables
- **Younger Scotch, IPA, No 3**
- Leeds

When electric lighting came to Leeds in the 1880s, Whitelocks was one of the first buildings to use it. It was a period of refurbishment for this splendid pub following its acquisition by the Whitelock family. Later it was restored again and recent work has retained all its high Edwardian grandeur. This is the city's best known and best loved pub. John Betjeman called it "the very heart of Leeds.'

All the bustle of the big shops and traffic of Briggate vanishes when you enter Turks Head Yard and see the splendid glass and brass of the windows together with the hanging baskets and lamps that welcome you to Whitelocks. Inside the joys are multiplied from the long tiled frontage and brass top of the bar to the dark wood partitions and the ancient settles. Old breweries are celebrated and ancient price lists are engraved on the mirrors. Everything fits, including the tiny restaurant at the top end of the room where traditional food prevails – pies, chops and steaks followed by puddings straight from the nursery such as jam roly poly and spotted dick.

The yard is a popular drinking area and a sun trap; further up is an overflow bar known as Ma Gamps which, though modern, has been done in style. The service in the restaurant and bar is friendly and swift and the lack of music makes this a pub to talk in. It was once the haunt of the artistic and business community of Leeds and now happily settles for a cosmopolitan crowd including many regulars and folk who return with regularity from all parts of the globe.

Wrens

61a New Briggate

✕ lunchtime and evening

Ind Coope Burton Ale; Tetley Mild, Bitter; occasional guest beers

Leeds

The Wrens is essentially a theatre pub. It was developed by Mr Wren in the mid-Victorian era to serve the Grand Theatre which lies opposite. The name continues, a rare example in Leeds of a pub named after its founder. To this day the tap room and corridor are prey to theatre-goers and performers, particularly the orchestra of Opera North who are based at the Grand. The warning is out to take care around ten-thirty while Aida, Carmen or Salome are still taking the curtain calls.

Yet the Wrens is more than a theatrical home from home. It wins the local competition for Britain in Bloom with regularity, with opposition from the large stores, public buildings and the premises of the burgeoning financial sector who spend many thousands to brighten up the city with plants and flowers. Needless to say, Leeds as befits the greenest city in Europe, usually takes the national award too. Through the year the pub is a cavalcade of floral beauty, a none too easy task in the middle of one of the city's major road junctions.

It's a generous pub as well, constantly raising cash for worthy charities by various means. A quiet pint on a Sunday evening listening to the keyboard music and the gentle humour of Bert Gaunt will cost you a ticket or two in a raffle for guide dogs or one of the local hospices. But the beer is the real star of this house with local Tetley brews in fine form usually accompanied by others from the Allied stable. There is a choice of three rooms – a comfortable lounge, a popular tap room and, where windows once proclaimed Smoke Room, a no smoking room where clean air prevails and the beer tastes all the better for it. The food's good too.

LINTHWAITE
Sair Inn

Lane Top, Hoyle Ing (off A62)
Closed weekday lunchtime

- seats on forecourt
- at weekends
- **Linfit Mild, Bitter, Special Bitter, English Guineas, Old Eli, Leadboiler, Enoch's Hammer and occasionally other brews including lager and cider**

It will be fairly obvious that Ron Crabtree brews his own products in the tiny Linfit brewery behind the pub. His prolific output is never sacrificed to quality and each one of the beers has a style and value all its own. To say "try them" would be inviting a catastrophe but a representative selection will repay curiosity and interest. Ron claims Enoch's Hammer to be West Yorkshire's strongest draught ale with an original gravity of 1080. Enoch, incidentally, was the bloke who during the Luddite rebellions not only made the dreaded shearing frames but the hammers to smash them as well.

The Sair is an atmospheric pub with stone floors, coal fires, lots of rooms and marvellous views which are all very rewarding after the toil up the steep hill from the main Huddersfield to Saddleworth road. Ask Ron how the pub got its name and you enter into the pub's best talking point and this can lead into others. Old Eli, for example, was a former landlord, Eli Dyson and, yes, the folk of Linthwaite (Linfit) did try to melt lead by putting it into boiling water. Just up the road is a place called Blackmoorfoot and that's at the top of a hill!

DARTS

The magistrates of Leeds have earned themselves a place in the history of pub law by a decision they took in 1908. At that time games of chance were not permitted on licensed premises. "Foot" Anakin kept the Adelphi Inn in Leeds and was prosecuted for allowing darts, up to then regarded as a game of chance, to be played there. He went to court and took with him a dart board and a set of darts. He pleaded not guilty and in his evidence set out to prove that it was a game of pure skill. He was allowed to set up the board in court and threw three darts placing them all in the single 20. This was a Yorkshire board without trebles and an outer bull. He suggested that the magistrates might try their "luck". They declined but asked a junior clerk to try. He missed the board completely with two of his throws. Anakin then threw again scoring three double 20s. "This is no game of chance" said the chairman of the bench and the case was dismissed.

LIVERSEDGE
Black Bull

37 Halifax Road

- Clark Traditional Bitter; Old Mill Traditional Bitter; Stones Best Bitter; Taylor Landlord, Ram Tam; Tetley Bitter; guest beers

Some folk argue that there is no such place as Liversedge, merely a series of townships called Hightown, Littletown and Roberttown. According to the Ordnance Survey map the Black Bull fits in the centre of the triangle formed by these places and almost on the final "e" of Liversedge. So be it.

This is a busy, convivial pub where visitors are made welcome and the range and quality of beer cannot be bettered. There are no frills and whilst it was recently opened out it has retained a popular and comfortable snug. Worth a diversion for.

LUDDENDEN
Lord Nelson

15 High Street

- Webster Green Label Best

Up the hill, off the main Calder valley road and away from the "foo'it" is Luddenden a steep pretty village of great antiquity and in it the Lord Nelson, built originally as a house in 1634. It became an inn in 1745 known then as the White Swan and changed to its present name in 1805 after the Admiral's victory at Trafalgar. Branwell Brontë was a regular here and borrowed books from the landlord when he worked at the local railway station.

There are three rooms all with character and all reflecting the unspoilt nature of the pub. The tiny bar lounge houses collections of pipes and golf clubs and also a polyphone; a second lounge is well furnished and comfortable and the tap room is splendid and all that is expected with pub games, atmosphere and conversation.

OSSETT
Crown

Tel: (0924) 272495
Horbury Road

- lunchtime (not Sun)
- patio
- Tetley Mild, Bitter

This is a popular stone-built traditional pub in a typical West Riding terrace. The main lounge is a cheerful place with wood panelling and a collection of dolls in a cabinet. Other rooms lead off and Ring the Bull is played in one of them. It is well patronised for its food; giant Yorkshire puddings filled with beef stew are a speciality of the house. In summer barbecues are held on the patio behind the pub. Accommodation is available in an adjoining building with five rooms of various sizes.

PONTEFRACT
Tap & Spile

Horsefair

✕ lunchtime

Cameron Traditional Bitter, Strongarm Premium; guest beers

⇌ Pontefract (Monkhill or Baghill)

This is one of the burgeoning list of Cameron's free houses which sell anything up to a dozen guest beers alongside their own. It was previously a disco pub and before that had a handful of owners. Presently it seems popular and settled and a friendly atmosphere prevails. The one long room with the bar running most of the way along its right side is broken into nooks and crannies, alcoves and a quieter lounge area to the front. Food is basic, mainly something and chips, but cheap and bountiful. Folk sessions are held on Wednesdays.

RIPPONDEN
Bridge Inn

Tel: (0422) 822595
Priest Lane

✕ lunchtime and evening (not Sun)

Ruddles Best Bitter; Taylor Golden Best, Best Bitter

This ancient inn is thought to have been in existence since the early fourteenth century and there is plenty of evidence of great age. The magnificent timber structure of the interior creates its own atmosphere. Daniel Defoe stayed here for a while around the period that he was writing "Robinson Crusoe". The location is pretty, with a pack horse bridge nearby crossing the River Ryburn to an associated restaurant.

There are three rooms, linked together but each on a different level. The furnishings are comfortable with some seating built into the stone walls of the window bays. The cold buffet is a popular favourite at lunchtime and includes joints of beef well done and rare, spiced ham, quiches and the like; in the evening there are casseroles, stuffed pancakes and some Italian dishes. It often gets busy for food and delays can occur.

SAXTON
Greyhound

Main Street, between A162 and B 1217, four miles south of Tadcaster

- lunchtime
- yard
- **Samuel Smith Old Brewery Bitter**

Nothing seems to have changed here for a hundred years or more. Stone flagged floors, tiny windows, wooden settles, coal fires and barrels behind the bar all add up to nineteenth rather than twentieth century. Let us hope it will prevail into the twenty-first. The bar is tiny and comfortable (comfy is a better word) and on winter evenings with the fire blazing there can be no cosier spot. Behind is a snug which the cricket club manage to squeeze into for their after match celebrations and at the end of the building is a tap room with darts, dominoes and even Devil amongst the Tailors.

Saxton is a place of great antiquity and has a magnificent Norman church that shadows the pub in its dress of climbing roses. Together they make great picture postcard material. The Battle of Towton, possibly the bloodiest in the War of the Roses, was fought just to the north of here in 1461 and in the churchyard is a monument to Lord Dacre one of the many Lancastrian nobles who died there. Lead Church, an intriguing structure in the middle of a field, with its three-decker pulpit is less than a mile west of the village and another mile further on stands Lotherton Hall, a stateley home and bird garden run by Leeds City Council.

SELBY
New Inn

Gowthorpe

- yard
- **Tetley Mild, Bitter**
- Selby

The New Inn is an interesting pub at the Abbey end of Selby's main street. It received the "brewer's Tudor" treatment in the 1920s and was refurbished again around 1950 when it was owned by local brewers Middlebrough whose "Selby Ales" sign can still be seen on the facade. Inside there are idosyncratic touches with coloured leaded lights, glazed bar screens and some stylised fittings. The front smoke room – known as the "Vatican" – is delightful; wood panelled with a bowed and glazed serving hatch to the bar. The two main rooms have style and an air of modest comfort. They lead through to the Stable bar which is mainly for youngsters but which fits well into the general ambience of the place.

SHIPLEY
Oddfellows Hall

125 Otley Road

- ✕ lunchtime
- **Courage Directors; John Smith Bitter**
- ⇌ Shipley

This pleasant symmetrical building has lost a bit of its style by the addition of a large signboard across the front despite the fact that the name is already well displayed. Its origins and intentions are obvious from this and the date of 1840 high above the doorway. The Oddfellows or Odd Fellows as the original sign says, were a mutual benefit society formed in the early nineteenth century. They were popular in the north of England and there are at least six pubs of similar name within the Bradford district. Upstairs rooms in pubs, and there is one here, were used for meetings by the Oddfellows, the Buffalos and similar organisations.

The large L-shaped lounge to the right is most comfortable without being pretentious. This is a locals' pub but the sandwiches on the nights of darts matches are handed round to everybody. Warm and friendly are the immediate impressions and it is obvious that someone has attempted to give some interest to the pub. There is a large collection of jugs and on the walls an assortment from photographs of old Shipley to prints of L S Lowry. The lounge has distinct areas including one within a large handsome bay at the back. A small tap room houses an assortment of traditional pub games.

SOWERBY BRIDGE
Moorings

Tel: (0422) 833940
Canal Basin

- ✕ lunchtime and evening
- patio
- lunchtime and early evening
- **McEwan 80/-; Moorhouse's Premier Bitter; Younger Scotch, No 3**
- ⇌ Sowerby Bridge

The Moorings has won more prizes than Seb Coe. In 1989 it appeared in the "Good Beer Guide", the "Good Pub Guide", "Good Pub Food", "Pubs for Families" and probably others as well. It is an excellent example of a new pub setting out to do something and doing it well. This attractively converted warehouse is at the joining of the Calder and Hebble navigation and the Rochdale canal and was built in 1790; but the pub only dates from 1978.

The conversion has been done with style, particularly in the main bar; the high ceilings have been retained with only the tall windows as new innovations. Together with some imaginative furnishings they give a pleasant, comfortable atmosphere. Families are welcome and a balconied room is available at lunchtimes and in the early evening. There is also a waterside patio, pleasantly attired with flora.

Draught beers are well kept and there are some 60 foreign bottled beers including many from Belgium, and a fine range of whiskies – Scotch and Irish. The food is good value both in the bar and the upstairs restaurant with such interesting dishes as Murphy's pie, lock keeper's lunch, Cumberland sausage made to their own recipe, and at least one vegetarian dish. Children may claim half portions or choose from their own menu; there is even a special drinks list for them with "cocktails" at 60 pence each.

Puzzle Hall

Hollins Mill Lane (off A58)

- ✕ lunchtime
-
- **Ward Darley Dark Mild, Darley Thorne Best Bitter, Sheffield Best Bitter**
- ⇌ Sowerby Bridge

This is the oldest pub in Sowerby Bridge, enigmatic in both its name and its architectural styles and retaining a tower that once housed a brewery to produce a local stout. The brewery was built towards the end of the last century to cater for the pub alone and in 1912 its owner, John Platt, fell to his death from the roof of the pub while carrying out repairs. Brewing ceased in

1936 when it was bought by the Wards brewery of Sheffield.

The pub is plainly furnished and there is a nice airy feel about the place. Traditional pub games here include table skittles and chess and there is a popular folk music session on Monday evening. A pleasant garden backs on to the river.

SOWOOD
Dog & Partridge

Forest Hill Road, off B6112
Closed weekday lunchtime

❀

Old Mill Traditional Bitter; Younger Scotch, IPA

A splendid tiny two-roomed pub known to all as "Mabel's" after Mabel Collins who is not only Calderdale's oldest licensee but its longest serving one. It was bought for her by her husband just before he died. This stone-built one time farmhouse is an inn of genuine old-fashioned charm. The place is warm and welcoming, the furnishings fit the style and are comfortable. Each room has its favoured customers but they do intermix and visitors are not left out. The pleasant garden offers some splendid views.

There have been some gradual improvements over the years, not least the installation of indoor ladies toilets. At one time they were outside and without lighting but there was the cosy comfort of a double-seater. The story of how a woman lost her handbag requires little imagination but to discover how she got it back is worth a visit to Mabel's to find out!

SOYLAND
Blue Ball

Tel: (0422) 823603
Blue Ball Lane

- ✕ lunchtime (not Tue) and evening
- **Marston Pedigree; Taylor Best Dark Mild, Golden Best, Landlord; Theakston Best Bitter, Old Peculier**

The old packhorse route across Blackstone edge passed by this pub and no doubt provided it with many of its customers as it dates from at least 1672. It has a ghost of a serving maid called Faith who was seduced, then murdered by a one time landlord called Iron Ned and there are tales of coiners, highwaymen and gamblers seeking refuge there in the old days. It is all very atmospheric and nothing in the present day pub takes any of the mystery and romance away. Today you go there for some excellent beer, good food and superb views.

There are two lounge areas: to the right a more upmarket room recently converted from some smaller ones; and to the left an L-shaped room with traditional furniture. On Friday nights you can listen and sing along to John Wilson, a winner of many pub pianist competitions. Folk musicians perform here occasionally too. Food is well liked, children are welcome and there is easy access for wheelchairs.

THORNTON (Bradford)
Rock & Heifer

Rock Lane

- ✕ lunchtime and evening
- garden with children's play area
- **Draught Bass; Stones Best Bitter; Tetley Mild, Bitter**

The Rock and Heifer is a little way out of the village on the north side, quite close to the Walls of Jericho and not very far from Egypt. Further clarification can be found on an ordnance survey map. The Brontës lived at Thornton, a village mentioned in the Domesday book, before Patrick was appointed Rector of Haworth and the sisters, Anne, Charlotte and Emily, were born here.

This popular many-roomed pub tends to emphasise the food side of the business but the other comforts are not neglected and the beer is well kept and served in a convivial atmosphere. Toad in the hole is a speciality here – an enormous Yorkshire pudding stuffed with sausage meat and smothered in onion gravy, just thinking about it is enough to get the juices flowing. There is a fish and chip shop here too, it was recently reopened to revive an old tradition. There is nothing pretentious about the food, simply good value and quality.

TODMORDEN
Masons Arms

Bacup Road, Gauxholme (A681/A6033)

- ✖ lunchtime and evening
- at lunchtime
- **John Smith Bitter; Thwaites Best Mild, Bitter**
- Todmorden

Until 1888 Todmorden shared its loyalties between Yorkshire and Lancashire and the splendid town hall spanned the river boundary – the building still shows cotton to one side, wool to the other. Despite the fact that the town's merchants made their money from cotton, it was to Yorkshire that it showed its allegience and that continues.

The Masons Arms is just out of Todmorden on the Littleborough road and is tucked away next to a railway bridge, close to the Rochdale Canal for which great efforts are being made to restore fully. Valley walls tumble down on three sides of this pub giving it a spectacular location. This is a well refurbished free house with a relaxed and intimate atmosphere, a friendly place. The lounge area is comfortable but the popular place seems to be the triangular snug with basic adornments such as scrubbed tables and a fine fireplace. The family room operates only at lunchtime.

Staff of Life

Tel: (0706) 812929
550 Burnley Road, Knotts, Lydgate

- ✖ lunchtime and evening
- at lunchtime
- **Moorhouse's Premier Bitter; Robinwood Bitter, XB, Old Fart; Taylor Best Bitter; guest beers and cider**

A splendid many-windowed building in the stone of the district, this is an idiosyncratic pub, particularly where food is concerned with three chefs producing their own special menus. It is just a few yards from the Lancashire border in the narrowest part of the wooded Cliviger gorge, overlooked by Eagle's Crag which has supernatural connections.

The long narrow interior houses a series of interlocking rooms with flagged floors, stone walls and beams with an interesting collection of bedpans and brewery advertisements. The small upstairs restaurant specialises in seafood and the bar meals are hearty, the separate menu of vegetarian dishes being particularly popular. The owner has opened the small Robinwood brewery nearby and this is proving very successful. His full range of beers are sold in the Staff of Life.

UPPER HOPTON
Travellers Rest

Hopton Lane

- lunchtime
- **Tetley Mild, Bitter**
- Mirfield

This eighteenth-century hillside pub has some fine views over the Calder Valley. It was once an orphanage and has turned full circle to become a Tetley Wayfarer's Inn where children have special facilities. The family room has blackboards, books and video games and children can either have half portions off the main menu or choose from their own. Outside there are swings and plenty of play space.

The lounge is warm and popular and houses a large collection of toby jugs and there is a cosy little snug. The good home-cooked food is predictable but substantial with steak and kidney pie a popular choice and many admirers for the well–filled crusty rolls.

UPPERMILL
Cross Keys

Running Hill Gate

- lunchtime
- **Lees GB Mild, Bitter**

The Cross Keys is an eighteenth-century stone-built listed building that overlooks Saddleworth church in that part of the West Riding that now has been claimed by Greater Manchester. The public bar is known as Buckley's Kitchen after an aging curate who lodged at the inn and, in a drunken stupor one night, attacked a woman with a red hot poker and burnt out one of her eyes. The "kitchen" has a excellent Yorkshire range, stone flagged floors, some good wooden furniture, screens and beams and all the things dreams are made of. There are two comfortable lounges; the larger one has a fine stone fireplace. Outside is an attractive flagged terrace and a variety of activities for children. A good choice of food is available.

This is an active pub and throughout can be seen pictures of its customers' activities – folk dancing, road running, fell racing and hill tramping – there's clog dancing and jazz on Mondays and the folk club meets on Wednesdays. It is also the headquarters of the local mountain rescue team.

WAKEFIELD
Beer Engine
Westgate

- ✕ lunchtime (Tue – Fri)
- ●
- **Ind Coope Burton Ale; Old Mill Traditional Bitter; Taylor Landlord; Tetley Bitter; guest beers and ciders**
- ⇌ Wakefield (Westgate)

Bob Hunter, a CAMRA stalwart, has transformed what was a nonedescript Wilson pub into a briskly busy real alehouse in an authentic Victorian style. Westgate is awash with good pubs (qv) and another one adds to the variety without detracting from the quality.

The main drinking area is stone-flagged and gas-lit and a good example of how sensitive renovations can be done. The wooden seating is good quality and the decorative scheme fits well with some old prints and photographs and a wealth of breweriana. There are open fires from some excellent fireplaces and further heat comes from an ornate radiator. Some snob screens add to the decorations without having any useful purpose and a door to the "Select Room" takes you to the domino corner. The whole theme is well done and traditional food such as spicy sausage casserole and bowls of hot chilli are most welcome.

Elephant & Castle
Tel: (0924) 376610
Westgate

- ✕ all day (not Sat eve or Sun)
- **Courage Directors; John Smith Bitter, Magnet**
- ⇌ Wakefield (Westgate)

What a welcoming sight this must be to many thirsty travellers arriving by train in the "Merrie City", with its impressive terracotta front proclaiming its onetime ownership by Warwicks of Boroughbridge. The windows deserve a second glance, for they are examples of real craftmanship with bevelled panes and classic shapes.

The entrance takes you into the large L-shaped lounge which is broken up into several sections. To the left is an area dominated by a magnificent fireplace in slate, cast iron and tiling and overlooked by a window from the Tadcaster brewery offices as decoration rather than for its original purpose. On the right a smaller area has some plywood backed settles and excellent bentwood stools and a collection of interesting framed documents. A modern piano stands incongruously in one corner but provides a welcome change from canned music. Behind the bar is a small games room with a pool table and "lean-on" seating. They specialise in pizzas during the food sessions with a dozen or so different toppings and a take-out service. Bed and breakfast is available.

Henry Boons

132 Westgate

- ✕ lunchtime
- **Clark Traditional Bitter, Hammerhead, GSB, Wakefield Ale; Taylor Landlord; Tetley Bitter; guest beers and cider**
- ⇌ Wakefield (Westgate)

Wakefield's Westgate station is a good dropping off point for HM Prison, Clarks Brewery and several good pubs including Henry Boons. This is the "tap" for the brewery and makes up one-third of the tied estate. The return of Clarks to brewing after an all too long gap was greeted with delight after the brew was sampled and this continued, as it remained consistently good.

Henry Boons is the perfect setting for fine ales; it is the quintessential ale house with wooden and flagged floors, some fine wood screens and glass and an old fashioned atmosphere. The side entrance is blessed by a wonderfully preserved mosaic tiled floor showing the bowing courtier of the former Melbourne brewery. This leads into the basic but friendly tap room decorated with "designer" wallpaper showing off the firm's press cuttings. The main bar is on two levels with the higher section offering a certain amount of privacy. There is good jazz here regularly. In what was once a yard is "Boon's Yard", a separate bar displaying a wonderful collection of old brewing memorablia. Boons has a high reputation for food.

Redoubt

28 Horbury Road

Tetley Mild, Bitter

Wakefield (Westgate)

Let's start with what you won't find in the Redoubt. There is no garden, family room, accommodation or meals. What you will find is a lot of atmosphere in an unspoilt Victorian local; a perfect example of the West Riding "domestic" style of pub which developed out of the private house. Four rooms are linked by a corridor drinking area all serviced by a tiny bar. This is an unpretentious pub exemplified by its simple exterior but there are some attractive touches, particularly the glasswork in the bar. It fully justifies its inclusion in the list of Tetley Heritage Inns.

There are strong rugby league influences here with three of the rooms containing photographs and mementoes of the game. The other room has photographic evidence of an attack on it by a police car that ran out of control and broke through the walls. It takes its name from a warship which was itself named after the entrenchments used by the artillery in the Crimean war. But it had earlier names including the Spotted Cow and the Drovers Inn.

WENTBRIDGE
Blue Bell

Old Great North Road

- ✗ lunchtime and evening
- ▪
- ◎
- ⊕ **Taylor Best Bitter, Landlord; Tetley Mild, Bitter**

This used to be coaching country with dozens passing along the Great North Road every day and the inns competing fiercely for the trade. The Blue Bell claims to be the oldest house on the road. There used to be a sign displayed inside that had a date of 1633 on it but it could have been much older, dating back into the previous century. For a period it lost its licence for harbouring poachers (no doubt taking their fill of deer from the nearby Barnsdale forest). Now the A1 soars by high above and the Blue Bell and the picturesque village of Wentbridge enjoy comparative quiet for the first time in their history.

There are several well furnished lounges, comfortable and smartly decorated and a family room on the first floor. Children are most welcome here with the garden containing a slide and swings and a separate menu for them. This is a favourite calling off spot for the car trade from the West Riding towns and the pub often gets very busy.

WIDDOP
Pack Horse

Widdop Road, four miles north west of Hebden Bridge
Closed weekday lunchtime in winter

- ✗ lunchtime and evening (not Mon)
- ▪ forecourt
- ⊕ **Thwaites Bitter; Younger IPA; guest beers**

Hikers are welcome here – the Pennine Way passes quite close by – but leave your boots at the door. The isolation of this pub, which is in the middle of the reservoir land of the Pennines, makes it all the more welcome whatever your mode of transport. It is 1000 feet above sea level and on a winter's day feels like it, so the roaring fires and good basic food go down well. And so does some well–kept ale. Considering the position it is a bit upmarket and smart but loses no marks for that, consequently it can get crowded at weekends. The place is well furnished and the atmosphere, occasionally frenetic, is usually most friendly.

BAWTRY
Turnpike

28–30 High Street

- ✕ lunchtime and Mon to Thu evening
- **Stocks Best Bitter, Select, Old Horizontal; guest beers**

Bawtry was the ancient entrance to Yorkshire where the Sherrif would greet the King when he visited with a bag of gold. It was a most important coaching and posting centre on the Great North Road and the history of its inns include legends of Robin Hood and Dick Turpin. The town is now by-passed leaving a pleasant wide-streeted market town.

The Turnpike, which was once a shop and wine bar, is now the second tied house for the tiny Stocks Brewery of Doncaster. It has been tastefully converted and decorated and is full of interesting curios and prints and includes a collection of sporting caps and ties. It is popular with all ages and the good value meals include well hung steaks and locally caught trout.

BOLSTERSTONE
Castle

Off A616, ten miles north west of Sheffield

- ✕ lunchtime (not Sun)
- **Stones Best Bitter**

Church and pub stand side by side in the idyllic village of Bolsterstone with the sparse remains of the Castle from which the pub takes its name lying opposite. The present St Mary's church dates from 1879 and the stone-built pub from around a century before that. In a corner of the churchyard are – appropriately enough – two large stones which are thought to be part of an ancient stone circle. Along with the grave of a Saxon King some half a mile away, they help date the village.

The Castle has two contrasting rooms, a large L-shaped lounge complemented by a smaller tap room. Both are full of disparate memorabilia – stuffed birds, horse brasses, commemorative plates and old photographs. But pride of place goes to a large cabinet displaying the many trophies and awards won by the famous Bolsterstone Male Voice Choir who meet in the pub every Monday both before and after rehearsals. The pub provides lunchtime meals when children are welcome and has facilities for the disabled.

It is easy to be deceived by the quiet country setting of Bolsterstone and it comes as a surprise to find the Stocksbridge works of British Steel lie less than a mile away. The Castle provides quenching facilities for the steelworkers as well as for walkers who have struggled up the hill from the Ewden valley.

CADEBY
Cadeby Inn

Main Street, four miles west of Doncaster off A630
Open all day

- lunchtime
- orchard
- **Samuel Smith Old Brewery Bitter, Museum Ale; Tetley Bitter; guest beers**

This village inn was built in the sixteenth century as a farmhouse and its original beams remain. It is a charming place, welcoming and justifiably popular. A small bar room has pub games including shove ha'penny and crib and there are two lounge areas, well furnished with comfortable seating including a high-backed settle, and roaring fires in winter. A lovely orchard fronting on the village's main street provides an attractive beer garden for summer drinking. The food is of good quality and includes a salad bar and a carvery. The beers are always of high quality and 140 different whiskies are on sale.

DONCASTER
Mason Arms

Market Place

- **Tetley Bitter**
- Doncaster

This is the last truly traditional market tavern in Doncaster and one of the few remaining in Yorkshire. It dates from 1788 when it brewed its own beer and bearing the loss of that facility, little else has changed. The small front bar with its shop counter style and the small "stand-up" corridor give it a West Riding feel. This is a Tetley Heritage Inn and as such has been refurbished to a style to which the pub was accustomed. The lack of a juke box and fruit machines are not regarded as significant losses.

The front bar is really the tap room and the impressive timber counter and some delightful etched windows are its main attractions. It sports a racing theme as one would expect in this town, with framed sets of cigarette cards of jockeys and photographs of famous races including the oldest of the classics, the St Leger, battled out each September on the Doncaster course.

To the rear are two cosy snugs with a collection of photographs of old Doncaster with an emphasis on the market. At the back is a haven, a million miles away from the bustle of the market: a suntrap of an urban garden with its own dovecote. Keeping sentry watch on the outdoor activities is the clock of the former Plant brewery. A time warp.

White Swan

34a Frenchgate

- ✕ lunchtime (not Sun)
- if eating
- **Ward Sheffield Best Bitter; Vaux Samson**
- Doncaster

There were once 19 pubs in Frenchgate, now there is the White Swan and one can only assume that the best was saved for the last. This is a cosmopolitan pub, popular with young and old and a handy place to retire to after the rigours of battling through the massive Frenchgate shopping centre. Behind the narrow frontage with its beautiful etched windows is a small tap room with a claim to have the highest bar in Britain – well over five feet. You pass along a tiled passageway to reach the comfortable back lounge which is decorated with horse brasses and prints of old Doncaster. Families are welcome if eating.

DUNFORD BRIDGE
Stanhope Arms

Tel: (0226) 763104
Windle Edge Lane (off A628)

- ✕ lunchtime and evening
- in snug
- **John Smith Bitter**

This former shooting lodge is the home of the Dunford Bridge "Mole" Club, a gang of enthusiasts who take illegal trips through the now disused and adjacent Woodhead railway tunnel. They round it off with a pie and pea supper and a few pints at the Stanhope. The "moles" are said to be looking for more tunnels to investigate. Another claim to fame is that the reservoir that overlooks it is often used for filming episodes of "The Last of the Summer Wine" or "The Last of the Summer What?" as an American visiting Holmfirth once queried.

Irrelevances apart, this rather isolated pub still attracts a good deal of travelling trade from the Barnsley to Tameside road and with good reason. Several rooms are linked to the bar and there is also a tiny snug and a separate dining room where good food, including breakfasts, is served. It goes the whole hog in its facilities with a family room, disabled access, accommodation, a garden; even camping in the grounds.

It was once the hunting lodge of the Spencer Stanhope family of Cannon Hall at Cawthorne near Barnsley. The Spencers had lived at Cannon Hall since the 1660s but when John Spencer died in 1775 the line became extinct. His eldest sister Ann married Walter Stanhope of Horsforth near Leeds and their son Walter, who was the heir to John Spencer, took the name Walter Spencer Stanhope out of grateful regard to his uncle's memory. He built the hunting lodge which later became the Stanhope Arms.

ELSECAR
Market Hotel

Wentworth Road

Stones Best Bitter

Elsecar

Nikolaus Pevsner in his *The Buildings of England* series has nothing to say about Elsecar and its Reform Row but in its own right the village is as worthy of mention as Saltaire. And when Earl Fitzwilliam built his model village for workers at the local pit, he did one thing that Sir Titus Salt failed to do – he built a pub. And the Market Hotel is a part of the model village and fits well into its style. It has many rooms and a simplistic approach to the art of innkeeping: keep the customers, and mainly local ones at that, happy. There is no juke box, no noisy electronic games and, unlike many contemporaries, it favours beer to food.

Moves are afoot to make the village into a conservation area and to encourage tourism;

there are other attractions nearby including Newcomen's mine engine, a spur of the Dove and Dearne canal and, not least, the magnificent and enigmatic Wentworth Woodhouse with its 600 foot long front, although it's future is uncertain. Meanwhile the Market continues to serve the community as a popular local boozer but where visitors are very welcome.

HATFIELD WOODHOUSE
Green Tree

Tel: (0302) 840305
Bearswood Green at junction of A18 and A614

- lunchtime and evening
- Ward Darley Thorne Best Bitter, Sheffield Best Bitter; Vaux Samson

Here is a pub that looks at its best during the summer with its whitewashed exterior complemented by the well stocked gardens and hanging baskets. But it probably feels at its best during the depths of winter when the roaring coal fires add to its other obvious comforts. This is an outstanding roadside inn of true character.

The interior is divided into several rooms and drinking areas, there is a separate restaurant to which children are admitted and there is a large function room available for weddings, birthdays and the like. A beer garden completes the picture. Good quality and reasonably priced food is available in the restaurant and bar meals as well. The pricing policy for beer is interesting with all three bitters selling at the same price, making the premium, Samson, particularly good value. Service, as one would expect in such a place, is efficient and friendly.

The Green Tree dates back to the sixteenth century when it was an alehouse that later took on some posting business. On the same night as the battle of Marston Moor in 1644 when Cromwell routed the Royalist troops, a group of retreating Cavaliers found a Roundhead staying at the Green Tree and hung him from a beam in his room. Needless to say he has haunted the place ever since.

KILNHURST
Ship Inn

Tel: (0709) 584322
1 Hooton Road (B6090)

- ✕ lunchtime and evening (not Sun eve)
- ⊕ if eating
- **Whitbread Trophy, Castle Eden Ale; guest beers**

The Ship is the oldest building in the village, dating from 1752. In its time it was a coaching inn but the close proximity of the railway and the canal are sufficient evidence of the reason for the demise of coaching. The atmosphere is homely in this most comfortable of country pubs; for that is what it is, despite the closeness of major industrial sites. There is plenty going on here, with quiz nights and live country and western music.

Much can be said of the excellent food here and from me comes great praise for Yorkshire puddings served traditionally with just gravy, and properly made beef gravy at that. Other attractions include home-made meat and potato pie and a carbonnade cooked in Castle Eden Ale. Traditional Sunday lunches in the restaurant are very popular and it is advisable to book. The restaurant is open for Sunday lunch and for dinner on Wednesday to Saturday evening.

PENISTONE
Cubley Hall

Mortimer Road

- ✕ lunchtime and evening
- **Ansells Bitter; Clark GSB; Ind Coope Burton Ale; Tetley Bitter**

What started life as a mansion for the owner of the local engineering company has happily settled into its new existence as a public house. The original owner was called Cammell, he of the Cammell–Laird shipbuilding conglomerate, and like many of the worthy industrialists of the Victorian era, he certainly did himself proud. Despite some necessary alterations the house's best features have been retained.

There is a wealth of elaborate plasterwork, mosaic tiled floors, stained glass and original woodwork, all Victorian in style. And the setting in extensive gardens makes it a popular summer venue. Families are well catered for here; the pub boasts two family rooms. Other drinkers are not deterred and the popularity of the place is enhanced by some good quality food including some none too cheap gourmet dishes, with an interesting selection of beers from Clarks and the Allied Breweries.

ROTHERHAM
Bridge Inn

Greasborough Road

- ✕ lunchtime
- **Stones Best Bitter**
- ≢ Rotherham Central

The Bridge appears to be much older than it actually is and visitors are surprised to learn that it was only built in the 1930s. But there was an older pub of the same name nearby which went when the bridge was widened and the river diverted. The pub's sign shows the nearby chantry chapel on the bridge; it is one of only three remaining in England and is still in use. Like many other pubs in Yorkshire the Bridge claims a ghost, appropriately in this case, of a miner.

There are many rooms here each with its own character and this bustling pub is a home to many organisations and clubs. An interesting history of the town's pubs is displayed with two maps showing the location of pubs and breweries around the turn of the century and photographs of many long gone houses. A fine collection of glasses and drinking vessels hangs above the bar. Food is genuinely home cooked and the menu varies from week to week.

Portrait with pot plant

SHEFFIELD
Bath Hotel

Victoria Street

- ✕ lunchtime
- Small yard
- **Ind Coope Burton Ale; Tetley Bitter**

The terms of the lease of the Bath state that it shall not be used for the "...business of an innkeeper, publican or beerhousekeeper..." But despite this, what was once two Victorian cottages has been a pub since 1895 and took its name a few years later from the nearby Glossop Street public baths. It now takes its place as one of the most attractive small pubs in Sheffield and has been designated by Tetleys as one of their Heritage Inns.

The Bath is a tidy building where a degree of care has been shown in its design. The leaded lights are precise and together with the light fittings, the tiling and internal glass panels create a harmony. The main bar is functional with some interesting bric-a-brac including a timekeeper's clock. The back snug is delightful with curved seats, some nice antique tables, a hatch servery, a period fireplace and an Ind Coope mirror of the inter-wars period.

Cocked Hat

75 Worksop Road
Open all day

- ✕ lunchtime
- **Marston Burton Bitter; Pedigree**

Sheffield's brand new athletics stadium to house the 1991 World Student Games is being built right opposite this pub. It is just one of many improvements being made to this previously rundown industrial area, not the least of which are the entensive renovations made to the pub on its change of ownership. It is open plan with different areas to cope with pub games players, stand-up drinkers and those who want a bit of comfort and privacy. It thrives because of its cosmopolitan nature. The Cocked Hat has a reputation for its well cooked, good value lunches with a special every day. Friday is worth a diary note when, for £1.50, you can get home-made meat and potato pie with chips and mushy peas.

Fat Cat

23 Alma Street

- ✕ lunchtime
- courtyard
- **Marston Merrie Monk, Pedigree, Owd Roger; Taylor Landlord; Theakston Bitter**

Take a former tied house, add some imaginative but simple decorations and furnishings, sell well–kept beer and provide good value food and you have a success on your hands. There are, of course, other considerations, including coal fires in cold weather, the lack of a juke box, a no smoking room and an attractive courtyard with fairy lights for summer evenings. But the mix is excellent for what was Sheffield's first real ale free house.

The range of beer remains reasonably constant and there are ever changing guest beers alongside some Belgium beers in bottle, organic wines, country wines and a farm cider. A small but ornate central bar serves the lounge and corridor off which is the no smoking lounge. There is also an upstairs room which is available for meetings and often used to cope with overspill. The food is good and cheap; it includes some vegetarian dishes and a Sunday roast.

They play crib here which fits in well with the relaxed atmosphere. Families are welcome in the yard and the pub is near to the Kelham Island industrial museum.

Red House

168 Solly Street
Open all day

- ✕ until 7.30 pm Mon to Sat
- **Ward Darley Thorne Best Bitter, Sheffield Best Bitter; Vaux Samson**

The Red House was once popularly known as the "Irish Embassy" because of the number of Roman Catholic priests it counted amongst its customers. Nowadays it is a haunt of students and seekers of good ale. The star attractions on the food menu are giant Yorkshire puddings with sensible fillings such as steak and kidney, and some imaginative sandwiches such as liver and bacon.

It has been comfortably refurbished and has three distinct drinking areas served by a central bar. One area particularly suits the players of pub games which includes crib. This is a quiet pub with no canned music although there is live folk music on Sundays and quiz nights twice a week. There is easy access for wheelchairs.

Royal Standard

156 St Marys Road

✕ lunchtime

❀

☺ at lunchtime

⊞ **Ward Darley Dark Mild, Sheffield Best Bitter, Kirby Ale; Vaux Samson**

⇌ Sheffield

The Royal Standard was sensitively renovated in 1986 after a 12 year-old compulsory purchase order was lifted when the council abandoned a road widening scheme. Say "Cheers" to that and try the excellent choice of beers available in this pub close to the city centre. The landlord, John Elsey, takes a great pride in his beer and he has a regular of 45 years standing as his "official beer taster".

The pub remains basically the same since it was rebuilt in the 1920s with the original oak bar and panelling. The lounge on the right is in Edwardian style; there is quiet snug and on the left is the tap room with its selection of pub games. The pub is very active in local pool, darts and football leagues. At the rear is an attractive walled garden and another room upstairs can be used for meetings and functions.

White Lion

London Road

Ind Coope Burton Ale; Tetley Mild, Bitter

The superb leaded-light windows of this simple shop-front type pub on one of Sheffield's main arteries give you some idea of the delights to savour inside. This is a Tetley Heritage Inn and it is easy to understand why. Four small rooms are fed from a central corridor with the main bulk of the bar in the uniquely named bagatelle (or tap) room. All the rooms have character and their names are etched into glass panels – brilliant examples of the Victorian glaziers' art.

The corridor, lined with original ceramic tiles and some elegant woodwork, leads into a large concert room where regular sessions of folk music and jazz are held. It has its own bar and from here an unusual "priest's hole" connects with the bar parlour.

In the pre-Tetley years it belonged to the Duncan Gilmour brewery of Sheffield – a firm with a high reputation for fine buildings – and there is ample evidence of this including the window where "Windsor Ales" has an inverted "N". Despite its splendour there is nothing pretentious about the White Lion; it is cosmopolitan, simplistic and welcoming.

THURLSTONE
Huntsman

Manchester Road (A628)

Bateman XXXB; Marston Burton Bitter, Pedigree; Oak Old Oak Ale, Porter; Theakston XB

Here is a landlord who is prepared to take a chance. Bob Gosling's selection of beers would pass muster with any other in Britain and when Barnsley bitter made a reappearance from a brewery just up the road he was the first one to give it a go. It is the only pub to have won two Pub of the Season awards from the local CAMRA branch and its reputation for the range and quality of its beers is widely spread.

Thurlstone is a traditional wool weaving village and many of the old weavers' cottages, with their distinctive windows, can still be seen. The Huntsman was originally three cottages – two formed the original pub as far back as 1873 and the third was added in 1979. The original oak beams have been retained. As well as keeping good beer Mr Gosling's other love is jazz, so expect the odd session.

WENTWORTH
George & Dragon

Main Street, three miles from M1 junction 36

- ✕ lunchtime
- courtyard
- dining area
- **Oak Wobbly Bob; Taylor Best Bitter, Landlord, Ram Tam; Tetley Bitter; Theakston Old Peculier; guest beers; Scrumpy Jack cider**

This is a pleasant higgledy-piggledy sort of pub with steps dividing areas and an odd assortment of antique furnishings. An ornate stove dominates the lounge, a collection of blue plates decorate the walls and licensee Steve Dickinson serves up an interesting selection of traditional ale. To complement them his wife, Freda, turns out such dishes as grilled trout, venison burgers, home-made pies and savoury hash and nut rice. Kids are welcome at lunchtimes if they behave themselves, and "hear hear" to that.

To some the name Dickinson will ring a bell, for it was Steve's mother, Margaret, the previous licensee, who started the marvellous food business, Hoober Fayre. She has now moved away to a shop at Bawtry but still producing such delights as fruit cake made with Old Peculier and ginger cake with rum and Taylor's Porter.

WORSBOROUGH VILLAGE
Edmunds Arms

Tel: (0226) 206865
Off A61

- ✕ lunchtime and evening
-
- **Samuel Smith Old Brewery Bitter**

Before the building of the turnpike (now known as the A61) the old coach road passed through the village and the Edmunds Arms was a regular calling point. Worsborough village remains a small settlement with just the hall, the church, the old school, a few houses and the pub – it dates back to Saxon times. The road passes through the grounds of the hall and there were gates at either end well into this century.

St Mary's church is well worth a visit for its inscriptions and tombs, particularly that of Sir Roger de Rockley whose home still stands in the valley bottom. The inscription was removed by a vicar in Victorian times after translating it as: "He fornicated daily and was not repentant." The tomb was a double decker affair with a knight in armour on top and a skeleton on the lower level.

This is a superb pub as 12 consecutive entries in the Good Beer Guide testify and is a showpiece for Samuel Smith's. It serves good quality food and beer; there is a lounge, a tap room, a garden and a restaurant that opens at lunchtime; its situation is magnificent with a country park just down the road and an historic water mill nearby.

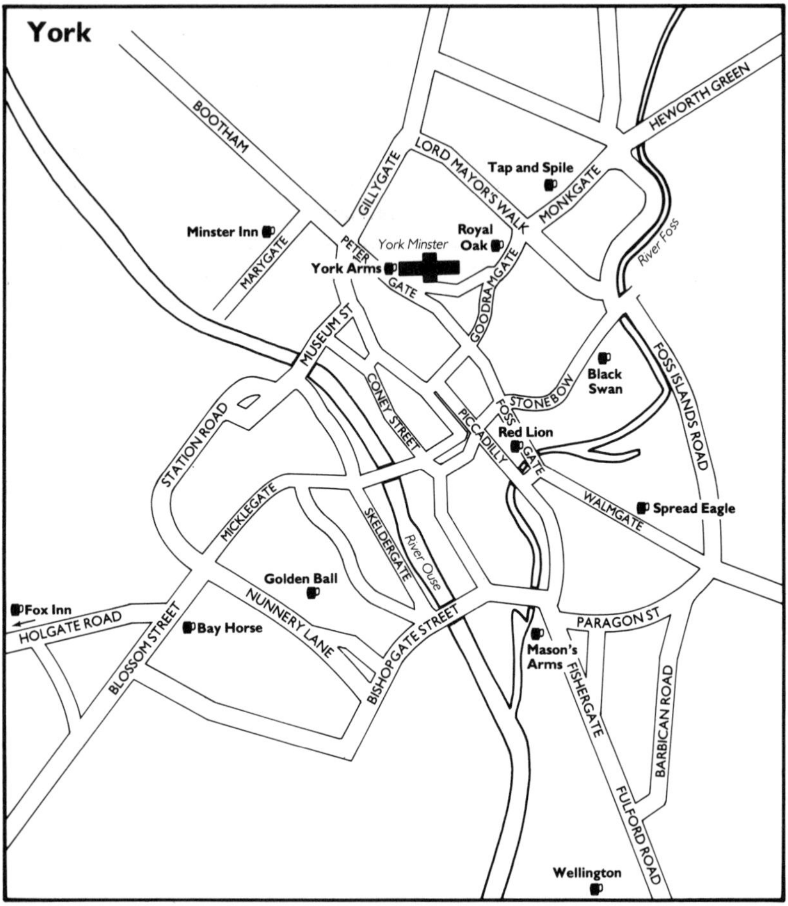
York
BOOTHAM
GILLYGATE
LORD MAYOR'S WALK
HEWORTH GREEN
Tap and Spile
MONKGATE
Minster Inn
MARYGATE
Royal Oak
York Minster
PETER GATE
York Arms
River Foss
GOODRAMGATE
MUSEUM ST
Black Swan
FOSS ISLANDS ROAD
CONEY STREET
STONEBOW
STATION ROAD
FOSS GATE
Red Lion
PICCADILLY
WALMGATE
Spread Eagle
MICKLEGATE
SKELDERGATE
River Ouse
Golden Ball
NUNNERY LANE
Fox Inn
HOLGATE ROAD
BLOSSOM STREET
Bay Horse
BISHOPGATE STREET
PARAGON ST
Mason's Arms
FISHERGATE
BARBICAN ROAD
FULFORD ROAD
Wellington

Bay Horse

Blossom Street

✕ lunchtime

❀

⊞ **John Smith Bitter, Magnet**

⇌ York

This small pub on the main road out to Leeds is interesting for its location. On this side of the city there are precious few outlets for traditional beer except in motels, hotels and disco bars. So a traditional pub comes as an unexpected treat. The Bay Horse is relatively unspoilt and retains a pleasant atmosphere. The bar in the lounge at the front is interesting from a decorative point of view and fits well into the comfort and slight eccentricity of the room. The floors are uneven, the ceilings low and there are some remains of old snob screens. The public bar at the back is smaller and basic but popular with locals. The provision of car parking is something of a luxury for pubs in York.

Black Swan

Tel: (0904) 625236
Peasholm Green

✕ lunchtime

☺

⊨

⊞ **Draught Bass; Stones Best Bitter**

The Black Swan is not only the oldest inn but the only one of several in the city that are listed as being of architectural and historic interest to hold a Grade II "star" rating, giving it additional protection against any insensitive alterations, or demolition. It is a sixteenth century building and was the home of the Bowes family which gave Lord Mayors to both York and London. Sir Martin Bowes presented York with its sword of state while he was Lord Mayor of London in 1545.

Although there have been recent refurbishments a magnificent seventeenth-century staircase, oak doorways and some panelling remain. The timber framed exterior is splendid with some carved bargeboards and was only rediscovered in 1938. In the eaves the original lead-latticed windows are preserved. The front lounge is comfortable with service through a small hatch. The larger back bar has a fireplace capable of roasting an ox and behind this is a snug also blessed with a large fireplace. Upstairs a function room is oak panelled with biblical scenes painted on the walls and a Delph-tiled fireplace. Food at lunchtime is straightforward and reasonably priced and accommodation is available.

Fox Inn

Holgate Road

- beer garden
- **Tetley Mild, Bitter**

There has been an inn on this site since 1776 although the Fox was rebuilt in 1878 as a boozer for workmen at the nearby railway carriage works and that provision continues to this day. A substantial renovation in 1985 left the original layout intact with the intention to restore the pub to its Victorian splendour and this has been done rather well. I wish other breweries would take a leaf out of Tetley's book and try to emulate the Heritage Inn scheme. The brick frontage has some decorative touches including a carved fox above the doorway. You enter to a corridor, typical of the West Riding despite its location, and to the right is the heart of this pub, the tap room containing the main bar. It is straightforward, with pub games predominating and perhaps an overplay on photographs but with a splendid stuffed fox eyeing a rabbit in a glass case above the bar. Hatches serve the corridor and the two comfortable snugs to the rear of the pub. These have many pictures and documents of interest on their walls. Across the corridor in which a noble staircase adds a good deal of dignity to the place, is a smoke room with darts and an open fire. The large garden has its own play area for children.

Golden Ball

Cromwell Road, Bishophill

- beer garden
- **Courage Directors; John Smith Bitter, Magnet**

As an example of a genuine local within the city walls the Golden Ball cannot be bettered. The unspoilt Victorian exterior of this street corner pub is most attractive with red-tiled brickwork and etched glass windows. Inside all the rooms are numbered, a throwback to the days of some obscure tax on drinking – something which has been the privilege of government down the centuries. The public bar is unstuffy, comfortable and popular, whilst the sitting room is where children and their parents are welcome. To complete the picture is a tiny snug just off the serving area. There is a garden here too, tucked away just where you wouldn't expect to find one.

Mason's Arms

Tel: (0904) 34985
Fishergate

- ✕ lunchtime
- yard
-
- **Draught Bass; Stones Best Bitter**

The location of the Mason's Arms adds to the attraction of this mock Tudor pub typical of the style of the former Tadcaster Tower brewery – the "snob's brewery" as it was called. It is handy for the Castle museum and Clifford's Tower and also for starting a walk around the walls. The pub's origins are medieval but it was completely rebuilt in 1935 with some original Tudor panelling left in the lounge. A gothic fireplace of around 1830 taken from the Castle gatehouse was also installed at the time. The public bar is plainer and popular with younger folk. The good value food attracts workers from round about and visitors alike. Bed and breakfast is available.

Minster Inn

Tel: (0904) 624499
Marygate

- ✕ lunchtime
-
-
- **Draught Bass; Stones Best Bitter**

A classic turn of the century hostelry which allows white-liars to say that they have been to the Minster when the nearest they got to the communion wine was a pint of Draught Bass. It was purpose built by the Tadcaster Tower Brewery in a terraced street that runs down to the river. Apart from other attractions nearby such as York Minster itself and the ruins of St Mary's Abbey, this is probably the nearest pub in this guide to the National Railway Museum attained by a footbridge across the river.

The tiled hallway is a good place to drink and you can then suss out the life in the taproom where darts and dominoes are important. To the left are two other rooms, a smoke room and a back lounge that was originally intended as a coffee room. There is bed and breakfast accommodation here and car parking can be found 200 yards down Marygate.

Red Lion

Merchantgate

- ✕ lunchtime and evening
- terrace
- **Courage Directors; John Smith Bitter, Magnet**

There are thirteenth-century foundations to this building and it has been a pub for more than 300 years. Its historic qualities are easy to recognise with low timber beams and opened up Tudor brickwork. A bread oven, thought to be 600 years old forms part of the front bar decor and upstairs is a priest's hole between two bedrooms with an escape shaft to a chimney. Being York, a story of Dick Turpin having used it is told, if not believed. A tale to sup a pint to.

The exterior gives an impression of being "mock" but is quite genuine Tudor, an expression of faith by its owners over the years. Inside is hardly touched, with alterations generally for the better. The three rooms are furnished to style and display differing personalities. The garden terrace is a oasis in the centre of York even though exhaust fumes do tend to spoil things a little.

Royal Oak

18 Goodramgate

- ✕ lunchtime and evening
- **Cameron Traditional Bitter; Everard Old Original**

This is a pub to search for, particularly for the day visitor questing for a fine pint and good value food. It stands between the Minster and Monk Bar in a handsome terrace of shops and pubs and seems to have avoided the attentions of lager louts unlike many other pubs in this area.

The former owners, Hunts of York, remodelled it quite stylishly around 80 years ago leaving a roomy front bar where traditional pub games are popular, a cosy lounge at the back and a snug which doubles as a children's room at appropriate times. Upstairs is a much used meeting room.

They bake their own bread here and that sets the standard for some excellent food. Roast beef and Yorkshire pudding is a favourite along with steak, kidney and ale pie, and there are specials such as pork chops in cider and Lancashire hotpot (yes, even in York!). Vegetarians are well catered for and everything is made on the premises, including the home-made pate.

Spread Eagle

Walmgate

- ✕ lunchtime and early evening
- yard
- **Draught Bass; Taylor Landlord; Theakston XB, Old Peculier; guest beers**

This pub has thrived on the real ale revival and recent alterations have upped its image somewhat and given it a fresh personality. The splendid frontage of this eighteenth-century pub is a reminder that it is only one of two remaining in Walmgate when once there were 26. The large bay window on the first floor is particularly attractive and the permanent features are enhanced by regular displays of hanging baskets of flowers.

It is a long and narrow pub with three rooms: a simple smoke room, a large main bar with a tiled floor and a tiny snug at the back. There is a grand collection of enamelled advertising signs throughout the pub. Recent alterations have included new toilets and better facilities in the garden. There is a good choice of food here and occasional sessions of live music. A nice touch is the list of beers available with prices and original gravities displayed both outside and in the bar.

Tap & Spile

Tel: (0904) 621473
Monkgate

- lunchtime
- yard
- **Cameron J J Hunt Ebor Ale, Strongarm Premium; guest beers**

This is one of Cameron's new free house pubs which until recently was called the Black Horse and catered mainly for locals. The York brewery of John J Hunt built it in 1897 and its facade of ornamented brick added to the streetscape of Monkgate. The change has not been as interesting as could have been hoped for but further plans are afoot. Meanwhile the atmosphere is pleasant with a light and airy feel to the place. The landlord is genuinely keen on the quality of his beer and he varies the range of guest beers after consulting the customers; as many as eight are on tap at any one time. Meals at lunchtime are proving to be a good draw. Handily placed for walks on the city walls and for the Minster.

Wellington

47 Alma Terrace, off Fulford Road (A19)

- yard
- **Samuel Smith Old Brewery Bitter**

The "Welly" is an unspoilt, side street local dating back to the days of the old Duke and like many another at the time it was named after him following his victory over Napoleon at Waterloo. It was purpose built in a row of working class houses which contrast with the villas of the merchant classes on Fulford Road. When the present owners, Samuel Smith, bought it in 1887 it was described as "an old established beerhouse", and that is what it remains today although the licence is more liberal.

My early memories of it are of wet, winter Sunday evenings tucked into one of the two back rooms in a steamy, friendly fug. Or of walking there by way of the river and Tebbut's betting shop on sunny, summer Saturday mornings and drinking in the airy front bar or the suntrap of a yard. Nothing, thank goodness, changes.

York Arms

Tel: (0904) 624508
High Petergate

✕ lunchtime and evening

🛏

Samuel Smith Old Brewery Bitter, Museum Ale

Here is a pub that offers good ale, good food and a ghost! What is more there are three disparate rooms and it nestles in the shade of York Minster, a next door but one neighbour.

There are two entrances to this smart looking pub which started life in 1818 as the Chapter Coffee House. The right hand one takes you into a tiny bar and a comfortable back room – should it be called a saloon? – and the other into a rather posh, more modern lounge which includes a "no smoking" area. It is quiet too, with no obtrusive jukebox.

Its ghost is shared with other buildings in the area and there are regular sightings of this "grey lady" – a nun in search of her child. Often she gets up to mischief, once showering ashtrays onto the head of a landlady and another time hurling a pair of bellows across a room. She walks through walls – well ghosts do, don't they? – and she vanishes if attempts are made to touch her.

The food is good quality, the beer is always of a high standard and there are some bedrooms to let. A pie, a pint and an Edgar Allen Poe tale before sleep?

MAPS

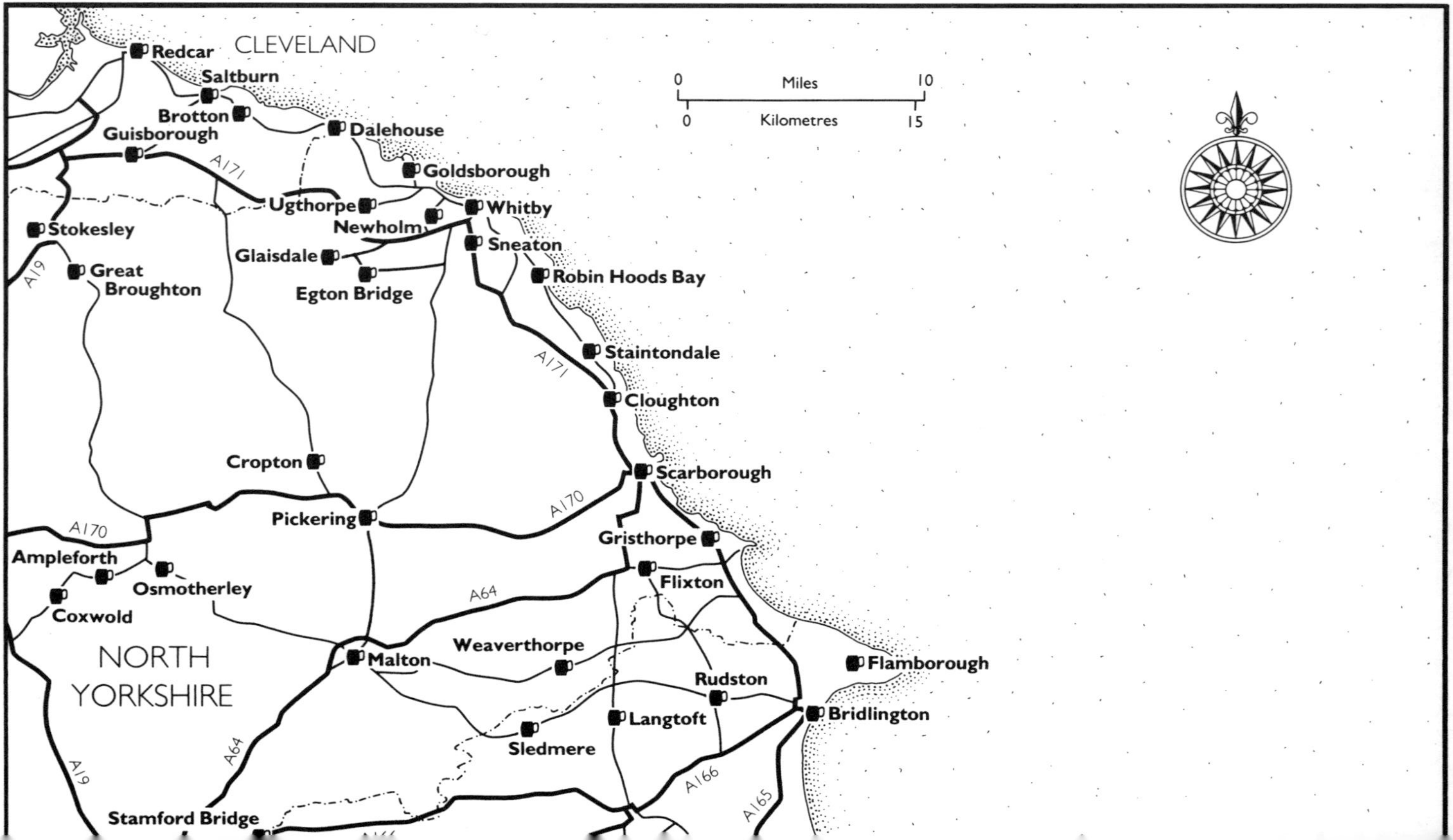
CLEVELAND
Redcar
Saltburn
Brotton
Guisborough
Dalehouse
Goldsborough
Whitby
Ugthorpe
Newholm
Sneaton
Stokesley
Glaisdale
Great Broughton
Egton Bridge
Robin Hoods Bay
Staintondale
Cloughton
Cropton
Scarborough
Pickering
Gristhorpe
Ampleforth
Osmotherley
Flixton
Coxwold
Weaverthorpe
Malton
NORTH YORKSHIRE
Flamborough
Rudston
Bridlington
Langtoft
Sledmere
Stamford Bridge
A171
A19
A170
A64
A166
A165
0 Miles 10
0 Kilometres 15

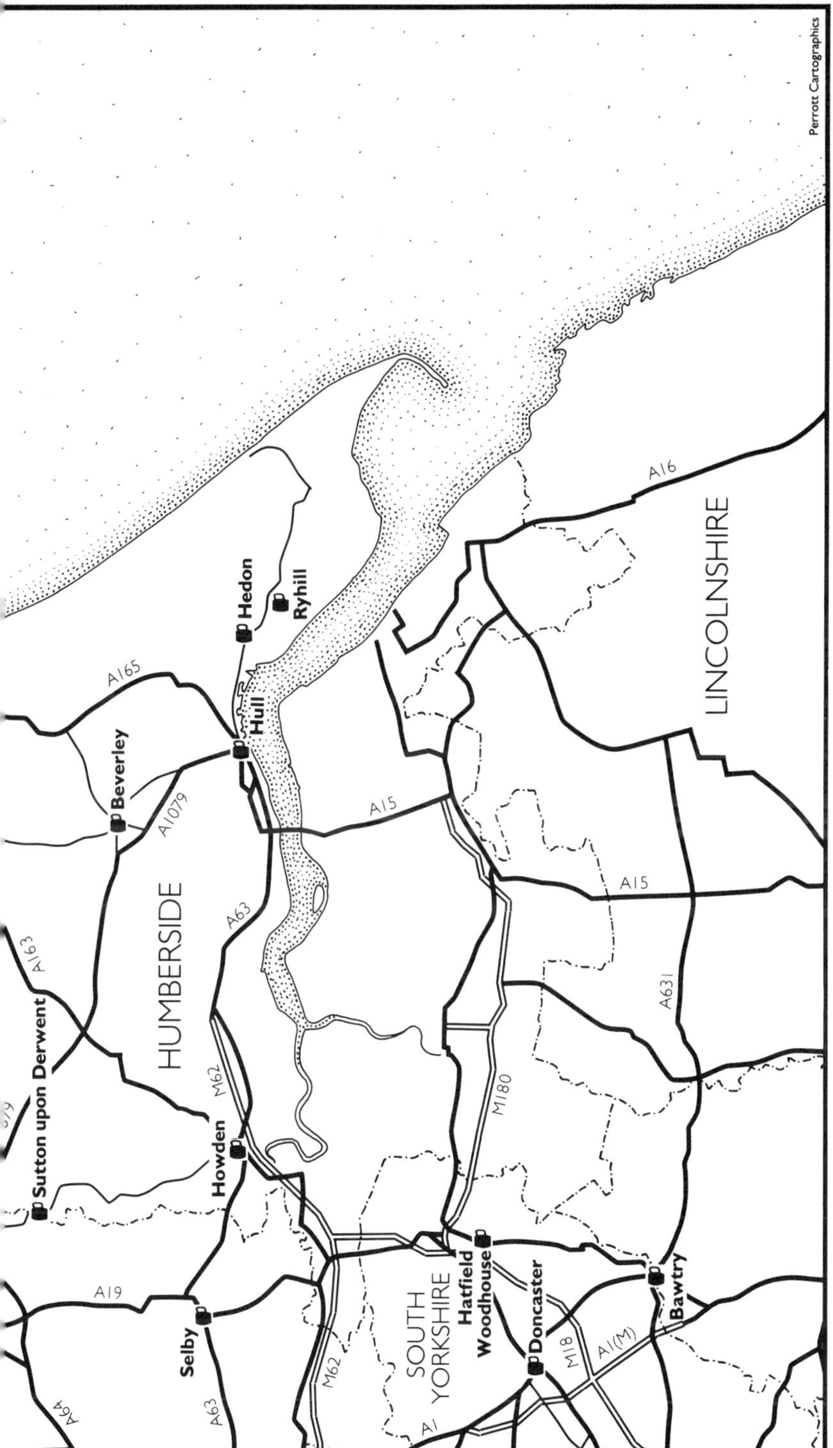
Perrott Cartographics
LINCOLNSHIRE
HUMBERSIDE
SOUTH YORKSHIRE
Hedon
Ryhill
Hull
Beverley
Sutton upon Derwent
Howden
Selby
Hatfield Woodhouse
Doncaster
Bawtry
A165
A1079
A163
A63
A19
A64
A15
A16
A631
M62
M180
M18
A1(M)
A1

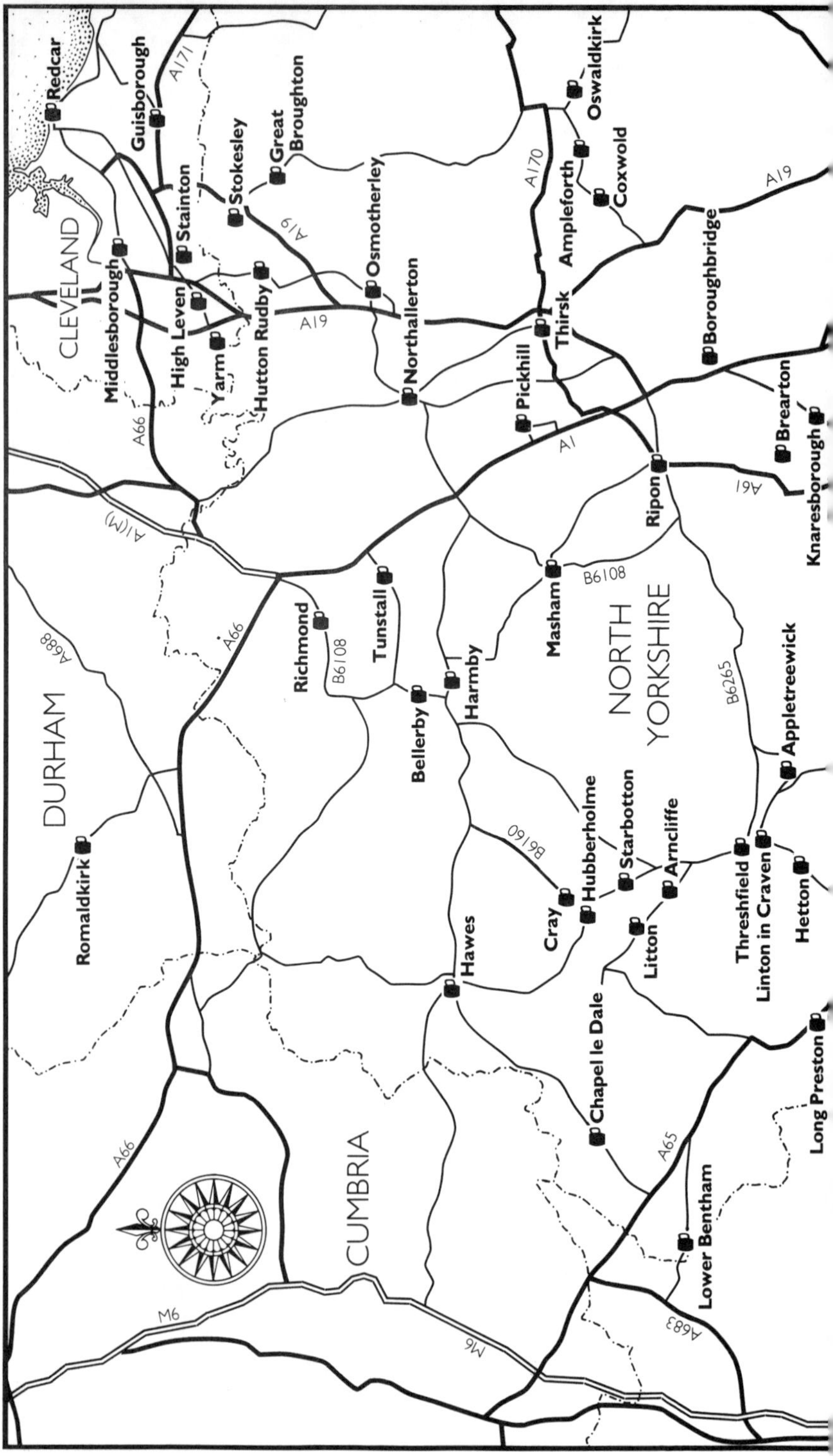

CLEVELAND
DURHAM
CUMBRIA
NORTH YORKSHIRE
Redcar
Guisborough
Stainton
Stokesley
Great Broughton
Osmotherley
Middlesborough
High Leven
Yarm
Hutton Rudby
Northallerton
Oswaldkirk
Ampleforth
Coxwold
Thirsk
Pickhill
Boroughbridge
Brearton
Knaresborough
Ripon
Masham
Tunstall
Richmond
Bellerby
Harmby
Romaldkirk
Hawes
Cray
Hubberholme
Starbotton
Arncliffe
Litton
Appletreewick
Threshfield
Linton in Craven
Hetton
Chapel le Dale
Long Preston
Lower Bentham
A171
A19
A170
A66
A1(M)
A1
A61
B6108
B6265
A688
B6160
A65
A683
M6

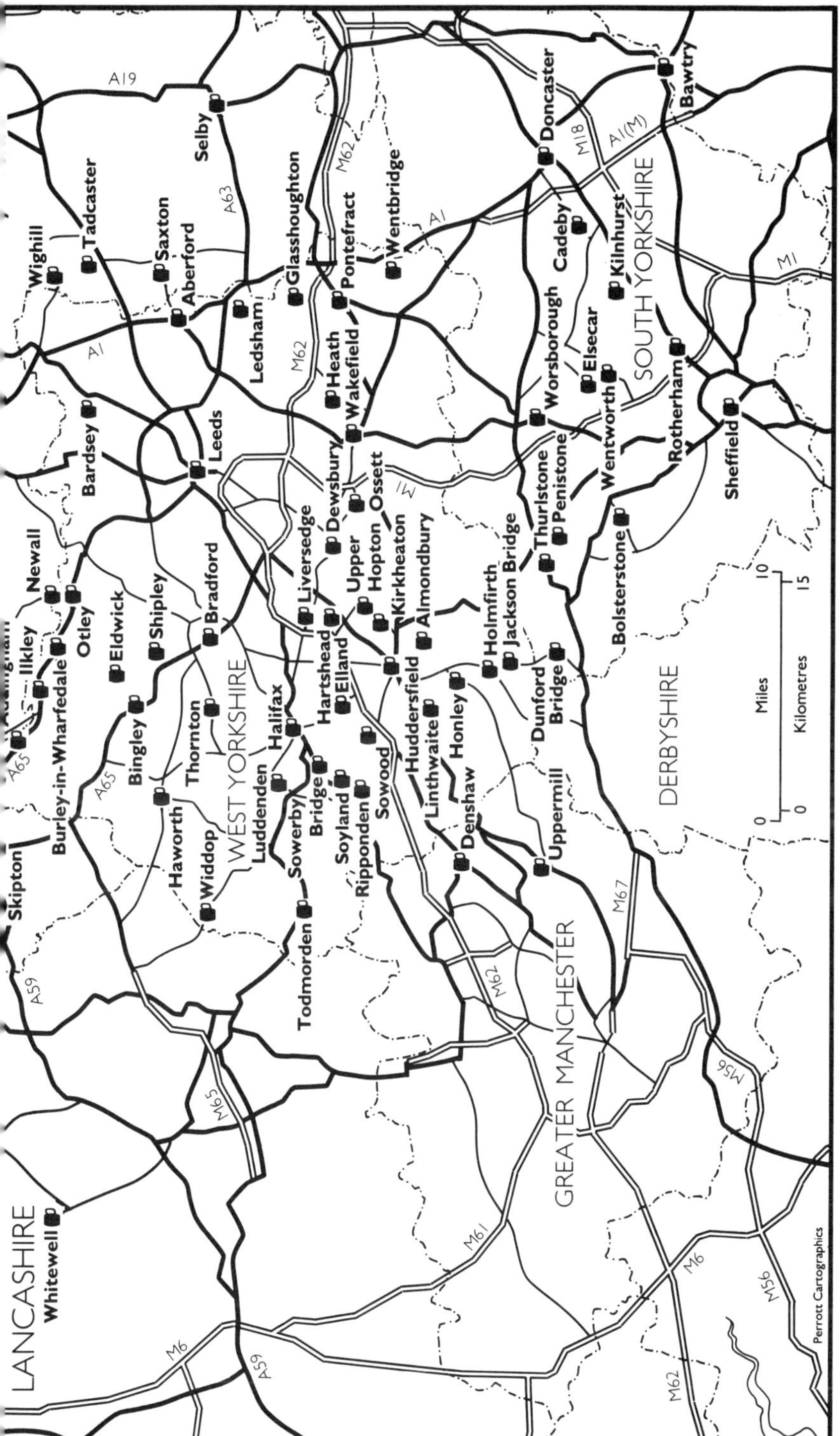
LANCASHIRE
Whitewell
Skipton
Burley-in-Wharfedale
Ilkley
Otley
Newall
Wighill
Tadcaster
Selby
Saxton
Aberford
Ledsham
Glasshoughton
Pontefract
Wentbridge
Doncaster
Bawtry
Cadeby
Kilnhurst
SOUTH YORKSHIRE
Elsecar
Worsborough
Wentworth
Rotherham
Sheffield
Heath
Wakefield
Leeds
Bardsey
Eldwick
Shipley
Bradford
Bingley
Haworth
Thornton
Widdop
WEST YORKSHIRE
Luddenden
Halifax
Sowerby Bridge
Sowerby
Todmorden
Hartshead
Elland
Liversedge
Dewsbury
Ossett
Upper Hopton
Kirkheaton
Almondbury
Huddersfield
Linthwaite
Honley
Holmfirth
Jackson Bridge
Thurlstone
Penistone
Bolsterstone
Dunford Bridge
Uppermill
Denshaw
Soyland
Ripponden
Sowood
GREATER MANCHESTER
DERBYSHIRE
A19
A63
A1
A1(M)
M18
M62
M1
A65
A59
M65
M61
M6
M56
M67
Miles
0
10
Kilometres
0
15
Perrott Cartographics

This ale, it is a gallant thing,
It cheers the spirits of a king,
It makes a dumb man strive to sing,
Aye, and a beggar play!
A cripple that is lame and halt,
And scarce a mile a day can walk,
When he feels the juice of malt,
Will throw his crutch away.

CHORUS
Be frolicsome, every one,
Melancholy none;
Drink about!
See it out,
And then we'll all go home,
And then we'll all go home!
Craven Churn Supper Song

ALMA BOOKS

Alma Books Ltd is the publishing company set up by CAMRA (the Campaign for Real Ale) to produce titles of interest to pub-lovers, beer-drinkers, tourists and travellers.

For more information about Alma Books and to obtain the books listed below (which are also available at all good bookshops), write to Alma Books Ltd., 34 Alma Road, St Albans, Herts. AL1 3BW.

Available now:

The Best Pubs in East Anglia **£4.95**
The Best Pubs in London **£4.95**
The Best Pubs in Devon and Cornwall **£4.95**
The Best Pubs in Lakeland **£3.95**
The Best Pubs in North Wales **£4.95**

Companion volumes to the Yorkshire guide offering the reader detailed descriptions of the finest pubs in the area.

Good Pub Food **£5.95**

Over 400 pubs around the country where good food is as much a priority as good beer and you may find some of the best examples of traditional British cooking, using the finest local produce.

The Best Pubs For Families **£4.95**

A completely updated nationwide listing of pubs which serve real ale, where children are not just tolerated, but really made welcome by providing good facilities including meals and play areas (indoors as well as outside).

Forthcoming attractions:

A Bedside Book of Beer
The Great British Pub

CORRECTIONS AND AMENDMENTS

Every year sees many Yorkshire pubs change hands. A new licensee can bring improvements or disaster to even the finest establishment. While most details were checked shortly before going to press, errors will inevitably occur and changes come thick and fast.

If you come upon listed pubs which have been ruined or if you find an undiscovered gem on your travels, let me know and I will investigate for the next edition.

Complete the form below or write to: Barrie Pepper (Yorkshire), Alma Books, 34 Alma Road, St. Albans, Hertfordshire, AL1 3BW.

County ______________________________

Town or village ______________________________

Name of pub ______________________________

Address ______________________________

Location (A or B road) ______________________________

Tel no. ______________ Name of licensee ______________________________

Description of pub (including bars, food, family room and any special facilities)

____

____

____

____

Beers ______________________________

____

____

Reasons for recommendation for inclusion in/deletion from the guide

____

____

____

Your name and address ______________________________

____

____

Postcode ______________________________

Join CAMRA

If you like good beer and good pubs you could be helping in the fight to preserve, protect and promote them. CAMRA was set up in the early seventies to fight against the mass destruction of a part of Britain's heritage.

The giant brewers are still pushing through takeovers, mergers and closures of their smaller regional rivals. They are still reducing the availability and diluting the quality of a magnificent and uniquely British product – real ale. They are still trying to impose national brands of beer and lager on their customers whether they like it or not, and they are still closing down town and village local pubs or converting them into grotesque 'theme' pubs.

CAMRA wants to see genuine free competition in the brewing industry, fair prices, civilised licensing laws, and, above all, a top quality product brewed by local breweries in accordance with local tastes, and served in pubs that maintain the best features of a tradition that goes back centuries.

If you are in sympathy with these aims you could be expressing that sympathy in a positive way, by joining CAMRA. We have well over 20,000 members and that's not including our three fully paid-up dogs and two cats! Yet we're pitting ourselves against the power and financial muscle of a multi-million pound, multi-national industry. We desperately need active campaigning members, but we are also grateful for the support of people whose only involvement may be to pay their membership subscription once a year. It's only £9, but each additional subscription helps us to campaign that bit more effectively across the whole spectrum of pub issues on behalf of *all* pub-users.

If you leave it to others, you may wake up one day to find *your* local brewery closed down, *your* favourite beer no longer being brewed. So join CAMRA and help us to prove that the most important person in the brewing industry isn't the megalomaniac chairman of some brewing giant, but that most vital, and under-valued person – the pub customer.

Full membership £9
joint husband/wife membership £9 Life membership £90
I/We wish to become members of CAMRA Ltd.
I/We agree to abide by the memorandum and articles of association of the company.
I/We enclose a cheque/p.o. for £9/£90.

Name(s)

____

____

Address

____

____

____

____

Signature(s)

____

INDEX TO PUB NAMES

Be not in haste,
Step in and taste
Ale tomorrow
For nothing.

Sign at the Chequers Inn on the Hambleton Drovers Road